For Jennie & Ro[...]

with best wishes,

Yasina & Shiraz

Jan 05.

SafariStyle

CONTENTS

First published in 1998 by
Stewart, Tabori & Chang,
A Company of La Martinière Groupe
115 West 18th Street, New York, NY 10011

Export sales to all countries except Canada, France,
and French-speaking Switzerland:
Thames and Hudson Ltd.
181A High Holborn
London W1V 7QX
England

Canadian Distribution:
Canadian Manda Group
One Atlantic Avenue, Suite 105
Toronto, Ontario M6K 3E7
Canada

Library of Congress Catalog Card Number: 98-85948
ISBN: 1-55670-859-9
Printed in Italy

10 9 8 7 6 5 4 3 2

SafariStyle

PHOTOGRAPHY BY
TIM BEDDOW

WRITTEN BY
NATASHA BURNS

STEWART, TABORI & CHANG
NEW YORK

DISCOVERING EAST AFRICA

By the turn of the nineteenth century, Europe had "discovered" Africa. The European powers were awakened to the potential of the vast continent by pioneering explorers who ventured into the interior for the first time. Britain's Royal Geographical Society sponsored a number of early expeditions to Africa, including those of John Speke and Dr. David Livingstone to find the source of the Nile River (eventually traced to Lake Victoria), and that of Sir Harry Johnston to survey Mount Kilimanjaro.

Scores of other explorers, map-makers, and naturalists followed, quickly charting the interior landscape, geology, flora, and fauna. What followed these finds became known as "the scramble for Africa," and Europe lost little time in carving up the territory, as this early political map from the archives of the Royal Geographical Society shows. The eastern strip of the continent was considered a particular prize because of its significant natural wealth. The British possessions included Rhodesia (later Zimbabwe) and British East Africa, which comprised Kenya, Uganda, and Zanzibar. Germany held Tanganyika (later Tanzania), and the Portuguese settled Mozambique. Madagascar, meanwhile, became a French colony in 1896.

Most of East Africa was colonized in the years between 1895 and 1915, and the impact in the home territories was significant. The "dark continent," as it was dubbed, promised mystery and excitement in an age when the naive and elemental spirit of tribal existence was a recurring theme in art and literature, and a popular topic for debate at upper class soirees. Africa became the adventure playground of wealthy and eccentric Europeans, who came to see for themselves the wild beauty, unbounded spaces, and cultural exoticism of this last great colonial trophy.

Kafa

Galla
Land

S.or Haines

SOMALILAND
ITALIANA

Gondokoro

Gananeh

Ras

Lado

Rudolf I.

Wadelai

BRITISH

Ingadoxo

Upoto

Aruwimi R.

Albert

EAST AFRICA

Basoko

Aruwimi

Nyanza

IBEA

1720

ville Stanley

Sta.

M. Ruwenzori

16600

Usanda

Eq.

Falls

Kismayu

ONGO

Alb.t Edw.

Victoria

M. Kenia

Nyanza

Nyanza

18400

Tana R.

E STATE

M.

Niangwe

L. Alexandra Nyanza

Kilimanjaro

19700

P.t Melinda

L. Alangara

Mombasa

Luhuaberg

Ujiji

Tabora

Pemba I.

1000

Amira

GERMAN

Zanzibar I. & T.n

EAST AFRICA

Bagamoyo

Dar es Salaam

L. Kassali

Rufiji

Mafia I.

Moero

Kasembe

Quilwa Harb.

Aldabra I.

Cosmoledo

Karonga

Rovuma

C. Delgado

Lohemba

Katanga

Comoro

Bululo

Bandawe

Mkalawiti

Is.

Nossi Bé

Shinte

Bangweolo

L.

C. An

Nyassa

L. Shirwa

Mozambique

RHO

Mponda

Mozambique

MADAGASCAR

Zambesi

AFRICA

Victoria

Lundo

Tete

Quilimane T.n & R.

Tama

Falls

Mashona

Sena

Antananarivo

Chobe

Land

Salisbury

480

8950

Tioge

Matabele

PORT. EAST

Sofala

Beira

Bechuana Ld.

Buluwayo

Land

Sofala

ahari

Limpopo

Inhambane

Protectorate

TRANSVAAL

esert

Inhambane

C. Corrientes

Fort Dauphin

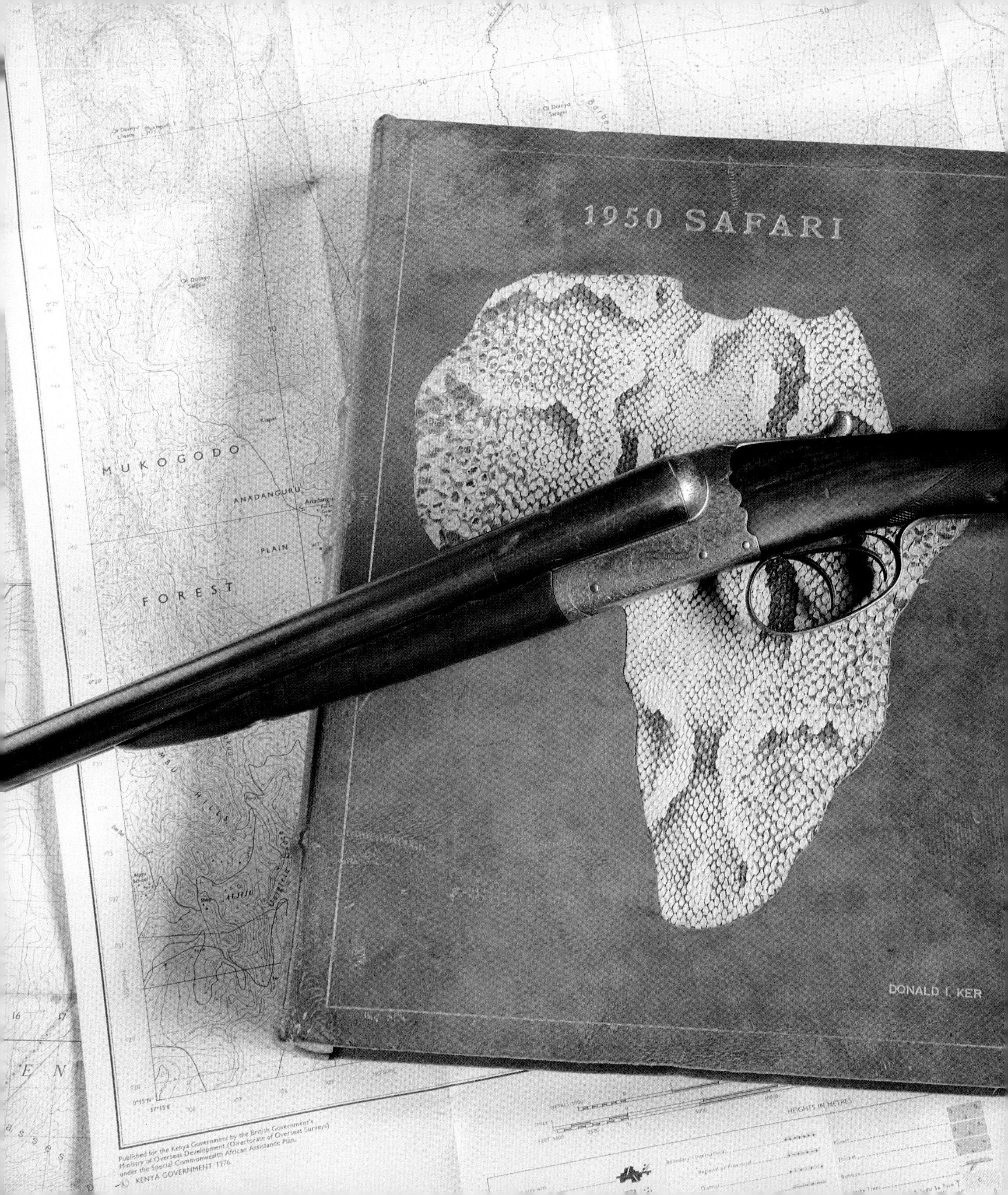
1950 SAFARI
DONALD I. KER
MUKOGODO
ANADANGURU
PLAIN
FOREST
Published for the Kenya Government by the British Government's
Ministry of Overseas Development (Directorate of Overseas Surveys)
under the Special Commonwealth African Assistance Plan.
© KENYA GOVERNMENT 1976.
HEIGHTS IN METRES

INTRODUCTION
ON SAFARI

ON SAFARI

More than a century after the first safari expedition brought Europeans into direct contact with the wilds of Africa, out of pleasure rather than necessity, the lure of the experience endures. Moreover, the imagery associated with the safari has in itself come to be symbolic of something more: The flickering of a hurricane lamp casting shadows against the canvas walls of a tent; soft swathes of fine mosquito netting shrouding a camp bed; a folding table set with white linen and silverware in the shade of a solitary flame tree; vast stretches of savanna turning gold in the evening sun; the pattern of zebra moving together on the horizon; and the warm glow of a campfire, beyond which the bush resonates with the language of wildlife. The travelers who captured these images, through their snapshots and writings, evoked a life of both pleasure and adventure, of elemental living in an extraordinary place.

It was the British colonists of East Africa who made the safari their own, spurred by a love of both sport and adventure. Out of the hardship of travel across difficult terrain in pursuit of their goal, they created an experience of great luxury and sensuality. This ability to imbue any environment, no matter how alien, with the comfortable elements of English living had already been well-established in India. There, in the course of building their empire, the British created a highly romantic way of life. They used native materials to reproduce the furnishings of home. They avidly collected the new and beautiful objects they found in Indian markets, whether of ivory, brass, or cashmere. And they perpetuated the customs of home—the institution of four o'clock tea, the formal dinner using fine porcelain and silverware, and the pretty decorative devices of Victorian England. As early as the 1800s, the British in India had

OPPOSITE & ABOVE

Early safaris were organized purely for allowing Europeans the thrills and pleasures of hunting, with local guides undertaking the tracking and hauling of baggage. The 1930s heralded a new type of safari—using motorcars, and for the purpose of taking photographs.

OPPOSITE

In 1923 Vivienne de Watteville set out on foot from Nairobi with her father, the Swiss naturalist, Bernard de Watteville. They took with them thirty porters and six donkeys on an expedition to collect specimens—elephant, giraffe, and white rhino in particular—for the Bern Museum.

BELOW RIGHT

Nairobi was thrown into a great social flutter in 1928 on the arrival of Britain's Prince of Wales, Edward VIII, pictured here in native headdress. He was accompanied by his younger brother, Prince Henry, who during his stay embarked on an affair with the aviatrix, Beryl Markham.

evolved an elegant pattern for living that merged the exotic appeal of local materials and objects with the comfort of the classic British home.

So it was not surprising that the first to establish the idea of living in high style in Africa was a British officer from India. In 1836, while convalescing from illness, Cornwallis Harris led a five-month sporting safari into the uncharted interior of South Africa. It was the first time anyone had undertaken such a trip, for the sheer enjoyment of observing the landscape and wildlife—virtually unknown to Europeans at the time; for the sport of hunting; and to record in his paintings the new world he encountered. During his expedition he also set in place a routine that has endured ever since: rising at dawn, a vigorous day away from the tented campsite, a lavish evening meal back at base, followed by cigars, brandy, and tales of safari exploits around the fire.

Africa attracted a stream of largely British adventurers and explorers as the century progressed. Accounts of their experiences, both in fact and fiction, as in Rider Haggard's *King Solomon's Mines*, fueled the fascination with the last great unexplored continent. In 1892, Lord Randolph Churchill, father of Winston, set out on a particularly lavish horseback safari across Zimbabwe. Not only were his hunting exploits much talked about, but also his extraordinary travel requirements.

Karen Blixen, pictured here outside her farmhouse in 1929, often left the comfort of home to go on safari with Denys Finch Hatton, but she made even the most difficult moments seem glamorous. In one episode, recounted in her book, Out Of Africa, *the couple shoot a lion at point-blank range, then calmly sit down on the grass to enjoy an impromptu supper of wine, almonds, and raisins.*

Early settlers were terrified of the effects of sun on both physical and mental health. A good hat, ordered from the Army & Navy Stores catalog, was essential.

Lord Randolph's safari entourage included four cooks, a surgeon, and a train of wagons loaded with "essentials" such as a piano, cases of gin, and crates of vintage champagne.

Inspired by such exploits, and by his twin passions for wildlife and big-game hunting, Theodore Roosevelt embarked on safari in Kenya in 1909. Roosevelt's priorities differed somewhat from Churchill's seventeen years previously, but were equally impressive in scale. Carried by hundreds of porters were the tons of equipment Roosevelt required, not only for hunting but for collecting and preserving the specimens he had promised to the Smithsonian Institute. Included for the president's personal use was a capsule library of sixty books.

In the two decades that passed between Churchill and Roosevelt's respective safari adventures, Africa had been changed dramatically by the pace of colonization. By the early 1900s some ninety percent of Africa was ruled from Europe, the British centering their colonial activities on the region of East Africa that would later become Kenya. Nairobi in particular, as the main British administrative hub, became the focus for Europeans and Americans in search of the high life in Africa.

It was in the hill country around Nairobi, more than anywhere, that the safari established itself from the 1920s as a driving force of colonial life. Although the word "safari" simply meant a journey, or trip, in the Swahili language, it was much more than that to the expatriate elite who adopted the term to describe their adventures in the Kenyan wilds. The safari was sometimes a necessity, for the purposes of surveying the large swathes of land handed over to new settlers, or arbitrating the disputes of the native Masai or Kikuyu who effectively became squatters on the new farmland. But more often than not the safari was a distraction from the rigors of farm life, an invigorating escape from the boredom of colonial existence, a reason to socialize. For in reality, the apparently exotic life of expatriates in Kenya in those vintage colonial years was in many cases very lonely.

LADIES' AND GENTLEMEN'S HELMETS

GENT'S CORK HELMET

Ellwood's	22/6
Hawkes'	27/6
Also for Ladies	22/6

CHILD'S PITH HELMET
Covered White Cotton.

Each 10/6

LIGHT GREY TALL HAT

With Black Cloth Band 36/-

COLONIAL HATS
Fine quality. Fawn shade.

Each.. .. .. 21/-

PANAMA HATS
With Black Band, Homburg shape.

From.. .. .. 21/-

BLOCKED STRAW HEADWEAR
For ladies' Tropical use, all the protection of a helmet, with the advantage of a millinered hat.

From .. .. each 7/6

LADY'S PITH HELMET
Covered White.

Each.. .. .. 19/6

GENTS' DOUBLE TERAI HATS
For Colonial wear.

From 27/6

LIGHT GREY BOWLER HATS
21/-

TWEED HAT
10/6

THE METROPOLIS PITH HELMET
New shape 12/6

CAWNPORE TENT CLUB HELMET

Each.. .. .. 12/6 and 18/-

FUR AND LEATHER MOTOR CAPS
From.. .. .. 14/6

CHAUFFEUR'S CAP
In Blue, Grey, and Green.

From	11/6
Cockade	1/-

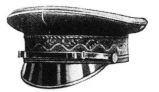

YACHTING CAP

Each..	12/6
White Covers	each 1/9

ALL PRICES ARE SUBJECT TO MARKET FLUCTUATIONS.

Social life in colonial Kenya centered on the various clubs and associations that sprang up to serve the white community. There were golf clubs in Nairobi and Mombasa, the Nairobi Polo Club, the East African Turf Club, and the Masara Hunt Club, among others. But the most popular of all was the Muthaiga Club, which opened in Nairobi on New Year's Eve, 1913, and boasted the best-stocked cellar in Africa. On race days, or for croquet, cricket, tennis, or polo matches, the colony's elite clustered around the Club for champagne and cucumber sandwiches. Evening events, accompanied by a live band, or the latest records played on the gramophone, dictated black tie for men and long gowns for women.

The Duchess of York, later the Queen Mother, on safari in 1924. There was much speculation in the press over whether or not the Duchess would wear shorts.

The majority of European inhabitants lived miles apart, scattered across the highlands that spread north and east from Nairobi, before flattening out onto the bare, seemingly endless plains. Dubbed the White Highlands in reference to the region's concentration of new inhabitants, the hill region with its fertile fields, cool evening breezes, and dramatic scenery was, geographically at least, the closest thing to home for the European settlers. But they also found the life difficult. The weather was unlike anything they had experienced, and the distances separating them from each other were far greater than they could have conceived of in their home towns or villages. And so, out of a combination of factors—isolation, boredom, and a sense of freedom imbued by their new surroundings—the expatriates developed a lavish style of life in pursuit of excitement and pleasure. For their excesses they became known as the Happy Valley set.

To their compatriots in London, Paris, Melbourne, or New York, the Happy Valley crowd seemed to lead the most decadent life imaginable. So confirmed was the image of Happy Valley as a place of abandon that a typical joke in circulation ran: Are you married, or do you live in Kenya? There was an almost constant circuit of parties, dinners, balls, tennis afternoons, horse races, polo matches, and safaris, all propelled by copious amounts of champagne, pink gin, and vintage wine. Most households had in residence a retinue of Somali servants who would lay the dinner table with the best porcelain and glassware every night. They had learned to cook in the manner of the best European chefs, and would stand to attention behind the diners, waiting to pour the next glass of wine or port. One old Etonian settler reputedly kept one servant on hand purely to mix cocktails.

One important focus of social life was the Muthaiga Club in Nairobi. On Saturday evenings, the Happy Valley set descended from the hills in their Buicks and Dodges, dressed in black tie and elegant gowns for a night of dining, dancing, and drinking until dawn. In between drinks, the latest news and gossip were swapped—the price of coffee beans, who was hosting next week's backgammon evening, and who was sleeping with who. Tales of safari exploits would also be traded—how the Prince Of Wales and Denys Finch Hatton had stalked an elephant for three days; how Kathleen Seth-Smith had been scalped by a rhino and lived to tell of it; and how Eastman Kodak founder, George Eastman, had amazed his safari party by cooking up lemon tarts, huckleberry pie, and an ostrich-egg omelette.

While on safari, too, the standards of luxury established in Happy Valley homes and at the Muthaiga Club were maintained. Essentials on any safari were rifles from Holland & Holland, pith helmets, safari suits, and boots from Army & Navy Stores, and hampers from Fortnum & Mason. For those that lived in the Kenyan highlands, setting off on safari could be a relatively spur-of-the-moment affair. Others traveled from America or England, lured by the glamour of Happy Valley.

Denys Finch Hatton was one of the so-called Great White Hunters who ran safaris for the rich and leisured. His trips promised spacious tents with eight-foot-high ceilings, fresh laundry daily, and hot baths. He also lent the security of a

RIGHT
....

In 1928, aviatrix Maia Anderson, pictured in goggles and flying jacket, became the first person to fly from Mombasa to Nairobi. The plane shown here, Miss Kenya, *was a De Havilland DH-51. It was bought by Lord Carberry in 1925 and was one of the first aircraft in East Africa. Carberry later married Maia Anderson.*

When Happy Valley settlers decided to head out on safari, the household staff would busy themselves with the necessary preparations. They would pack up silverware, crystal glasses, porcelain crockery, linen napkins, and bottles of champagne and wine into capacious wicker trunks. These would be loaded into a waiting motor car, along with tents, folding beds, tables and chairs, a bath, stove, hunting equipment, cameras, and other provisions.

first-rate marksman, should a rhino turn to charge (as it did the Prince of Wales before Finch Hatton shot it dead). But the most satisfying and most anticipated moment of the safari was on return to the camp at sundown, where cocktails would be waiting on a table laid for dinner with white linen and silverware.

Finch Hatton knew the importance of this magical time, and would always be well-stocked with wine and spirits for the occasion. A wine connoisseur, he traveled to Paris once a year to buy stock, not only for the cellars of the Muthaiga Club, but for his own supply, most famously shared with his friend and lover, Karen Blixen. In between his paid safaris, Finch Hatton would stay at Blixen's farm in the Ngong Hills, above Nairobi, bringing with him bottles of champagne and vintage wine, cigars from Benson & Hedges, gramophone records, and books.

Karen Blixen was one of the many new settlers who captured the great appeal of safari life. Her home typified the architecture and interior style of colonial Kenya in the 1920s. A roomy stone-built bungalow with a wide veranda and open hearth, it catered for both blistering hot days and chilly evenings. It was decorated with a mixture of hefty European furniture, locally made chairs with wicker backs and seats, and the folding tray tables and chairs of the safari. Although the furnishing style was much sparer than it would have been in Europe—to maximize the flow of air through the house—it did boast the dinner settings of a fine aristocratic home. In this, at least, the experience and habits of the Old World lived on in Africa.

Likewise, those settlers that left Africa to return home took with them elements of a new interior style, including many of the items associated with the safari—the folding furniture, the pale lightweight fabrics, and the African handicrafts. Even if these elements seemed improbable in their new northern environment, they lent European homes an exotic air in keeping with the times, a reminder of the pleasures of travel, of taking off at a moment's notice for adventures in distant places, and of the delights of living simply, yet luxuriously.

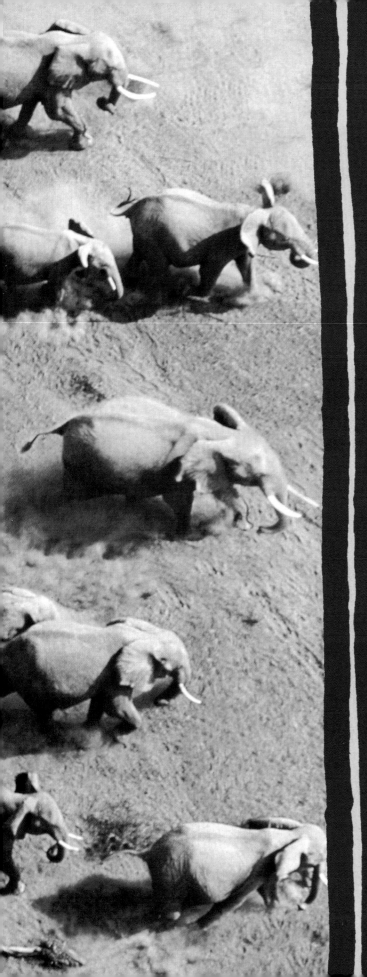

CHAPTER ONE
LODGES
& CAMPS

WILDERNESS ENCOUNTERED

The dramatic, rocky terrain of Tsavo East National Park does not conform to every visitor's idea of the Kenyan bush. Tsavo is remote and untamed, its wildlife boasting an extraordinary biodiversity. Red elephants, elegant Hirol antelopes, man-eating lions, and flocks of vividly colored carmine make the Tsavo their home, and tourism here is tightly controlled in order to preserve the area's unique mix of species.

One of the few safari facilities in Tsavo East, Galdessa Camp makes the national park's wildlife its focus. Camp founder Pierre Mourgue d'Algue works closely with the Kenya Wildlife Service on conservation projects such as the reintroduction of the rare black rhino. It is this close interaction with animals, as well as isolation from human settlement, that gives Galdessa its wild, almost primitive flavor. Guests are accommodated in individual *bandas*. Each of these secluded thatch-roofed tents is built on a timber platform, with walls of mosquito netting and canvas. Elephants, buffalos, and rhinos congregate just yards away at the riverbed that cuts through the camp.

Inside the banda, lamps fashioned from ostrich eggs, gnarled wooden headboards, and a bathroom clad in stone enhance the camp's sense of harmony with its surroundings. Creature comforts are equally important though. Each banda is powered by solar electricity, with hot water fed through a traditional canvas drum shower in the private bathrooms, and a field telephone links to the kitchen for ordering sundowners or freshly baked croissants. Particular emphasis is placed on the experience of dining in the wild. Evening meals may be enjoyed under the stars, while breakfast is served at camp tables by the riverbed as wildlife gathers for a morning drink. Few safari experiences in East Africa are as intense, or as intimate.

OPPOSITE

....

Set by the river in a grove of doum palm trees, the main camp "mess" provides a communal area for lounging and dining, although meals are also served in more intimate surroundings. In keeping with the philosophy of Galdessa, both the mess building and furnishings are in harmony with the environment. The roof is thatched with grass and the structure's support poles are a replenishable resource—native gums from a plantation. The floor is local Galana stone, and the dining table is made from a stone slab found in the national park.

ABOVE

*All eight of Galdessa's individual bandas
are spread out along the riverbank, but
the Rhino Suite, or honeymoon banda,
is the most intimate of all, located well
away from the rest of the camp. The
king-sized bed is made from wood found
in the national park and is draped
romantically in cotton mosquito nets.*

OPPOSITE

*The viewing platform and sundeck of the
Rhino Suite overlook the Galana River
and Yatta Escarpment. This secluded
vantage point is ideal for observing the
rhinos and buffalos that cluster around
the river in the early morning and
evening, or simply for enjoying a glass
of wine and plate of ripe mango.*

ABOVE & RIGHT

·····································

*Each banda sits on a floor of plantation-grown cypress,
with tented walls and a thatched roof. As with a tent,
the front canvas flap is zipped up at night but opens
during the day onto a sun-drenched veranda with views
of the river. Most of the furnishings are fashioned from
stone and wood found around the camp. Decorative
details come in the form of regional textiles and crafts,
like the glasses and water jug with Masai beading.*

The spacious bathrooms include dressing space, closets, and a shower room with a stone floor. Each banda is supplied with running water, but the shower itself is a traditional safari drum, which is filled by hand to the temperature preferred by each guest.

LEFT & BELOW

Rough bush textures give the bathroom a primitive feel. The stone basin is set into a stack of river rocks, and solar-powered lamps are made from Ostrich eggshells fixed on buffalo vertebrae. In a sunny corner of the room, a seedpod looks startlingly like a snake at first glance.

NATIVE ELEMENTS

From the air, the six neatly thatched cottages and mess buildings comprising Borana Lodge are barely visible. Even approaching them by road, after a long dusty drive from Nairobi, they appear as little more than shadows on the scrubby green hills of the Kenyan highlands. Clinging to a ridge in the Samangua Valley, Borana is the most discreet of safari lodges. Owners Michael and Nicky Dyer and designer Murray Levet shared the same vision for Borana: that it should blend into the surrounding landscape, while providing a stunning viewpoint for observing the area's wealth of wildlife.

The Dyers were captivated by this unspoiled corner of Kenya more than a decade ago, acquiring a 35,000-acre ranch near Timau, north of Mount Kenya, where they farm cattle, sheep, and camels. It was only several years ago that they decided to share their patch of wilderness, constructing a lodge compound that would accommodate no more than a dozen paying guests. The result—six thatched huts, two communal living areas, and a dining hall with wide veranda overlooking the valley—are intended to offer a homely and thoroughly relaxing respite from days out on safari.

In keeping with the intentions of Borana, almost every part of the lodge has been made by hand from natural elements. The huts and communal halls are built from fallen cedar trees collected from the ranch woodlands and local stone, with pitched roofs thatched with grasses from the swamps. Complementing the rustic structures, the furniture is crafted by artisans using Kenyan rosewood and cedar. The dining-chair seats and backs are slung with leather hides from the ranch cattle, and traditionally woven wools and cotton textiles are used throughout for upholstery, bedcovers, and curtains.

OPPOSITE

....

The private cottages are a showcase for the work of local artists. Fabrics and textiles have been sourced from all over Kenya, and are sewn up on-site by an old tailor with an ancient sewing machine. The cottages vary in shape as they have been created to fit into the immediate environment with a minimum of disturbance.

LEFT & ABOVE

....

Borana blends perfectly with the surrounding
countryside, high in the northern frontier district of
Kenya. The surrounding hills are wooded, but the valley
below is fairly dry with whistling thorns, acacia trees,
scrub, and some open grassland. It is ideal country
for game, attracting elephants, greater kudu, waterbuck,
impala, zebra, giraffe, and lions.

RIGHT

The largest cottage serves as a communal living area for
guests. The walls are made from chunks of orangey
sandstone cemented together with a mixture that
includes the deep red soil of the valley. The overall
effect is earthy, warm, and comforting.

BELOW

Like most of the furniture at the lodge, the side table in
the living area has been fashioned from a huge, rough-
edged slice of fallen cedar. Nestled on top are a clutch
of native pottery vessels and a decorated gourd
that serves as a lamp base.

LEFT

The roof on the main lodge building and
those on the private cottages are made
from reed thatch, which is twisted around
fine cedar sticks to give an interesting
knotted effect from the inside and a
typical thatched look from the outside.

ABOVE, LEFT & RIGHT

Decoration of the camp includes unusual
details reflecting the natural
environment. A painting on the dining-
room wall depicts the impala that graze
on the plains below the lodge. Handles on
a cabinet are made from knotted twigs.

SAFARI BAROQUE

The creators of the Ngorongoro Crater Lodge in Tanzania refer to its extravagant interior style as "Masai Versailles." This collision of African mud-hut architecture with Old World gilded luxury—all exaggerated by a fanciful sense of imagination—has resulted in a safari experience unlike any other in Africa. The lodge itself stands on the former site of the British Governor's hunting retreat, built in 1934 on the rim of the Ngorongoro Crater, with breathtaking views over the caldera. The astonishing natural setting makes the baroque-style decor seem even more surreal, which is perhaps just the effect architect Silvio Rech intended.

Directing a huge team of designers, African crafts people, and laborers, Rech worked in conjunction with owners Conservation Corporation Africa. One of the key considerations was the environmental impact on the crater, a world heritage site, and so the buildings were envisaged as lightweight structures, raised on stilts and made from natural materials. The resulting design is inspired by the mud huts of the Masai but also incorporates other influential African styles, like the wood carving of Zanzibar and the thatched roofing of the eastern coastal regions.

While the exterior vision is of a series of stylized native huts, the interiors are lavish and eclectic. Crystal chandeliers are suspended from ceilings thatched with banana leaves; gilt-edged mirrors reflect paneled walls of *mnenga* wood; and silk drapes are swept aside to reveal one of Africa's natural wonders. Despite the overwhelming visual style of the lodge interiors, the Ngorongoro crater is the main attraction, with both communal areas and private cottages arranged to make the most of the view. Whether guests are imbibing fine wines, lazing in bed, or soaking in a bath, the spectacular Ngorongoro is ever-present.

OPPOSITE
....

Architect Silvio Rech intended Crater Lodge as a vision of contrasts, evident here in the main dining hall where lavish European and raw native elements collide. The chandeliers were made on site by Masai tribes using crystal beads from South Africa. The molded ceiling decorations were also brought from South Africa but gilded by local artisans. The polished floors are of mnenga *wood, as are most of the other wooden surfaces.*

Three individual camps, each accom-
modating twenty-four guests, are ranged
at different levels on the lodge site. All
have stunning views of the Ngorongoro,
which attracts thousands of animals on
their migrations across the continent.

The lodge structures are made almost
entirely from wood—registered by the
forestry department to ensure it is sourced
from plantations rather than wild forests
—and mud brick. Roofs are made from
palm fronds, lined with banana leaves.

LEFT & ABOVE

··

Reflecting the diverse mix of elements in the lodge's interior scheme, the dining tables are set with antique silverware, originally commissioned for the restaurant carriages of Africa's early railways. Damask tablecloths provide the backdrop for polished silver, fine crystal, and iron candelabra made by Masai craftsmen. Two bronze Masai warriors stand on a side table—the bananas next to them are one of twenty varieties grown in the area.

ABOVE, LEFT & RIGHT

The high ceiling in the lounge area is lined with hundreds of banana leaves folded over a wire frame, and supports a crystal chandelier. The paneled walls were created by a team of fifty carpenters and carvers from Zanzibar.

OPPOSITE

The sofas and armchairs were custom-made using Mulberry fabrics from England, while the coffee tables were sourced from antique shops in Nairobi. Adorning the walls of a small alcove are old fabric-printing blocks from India.

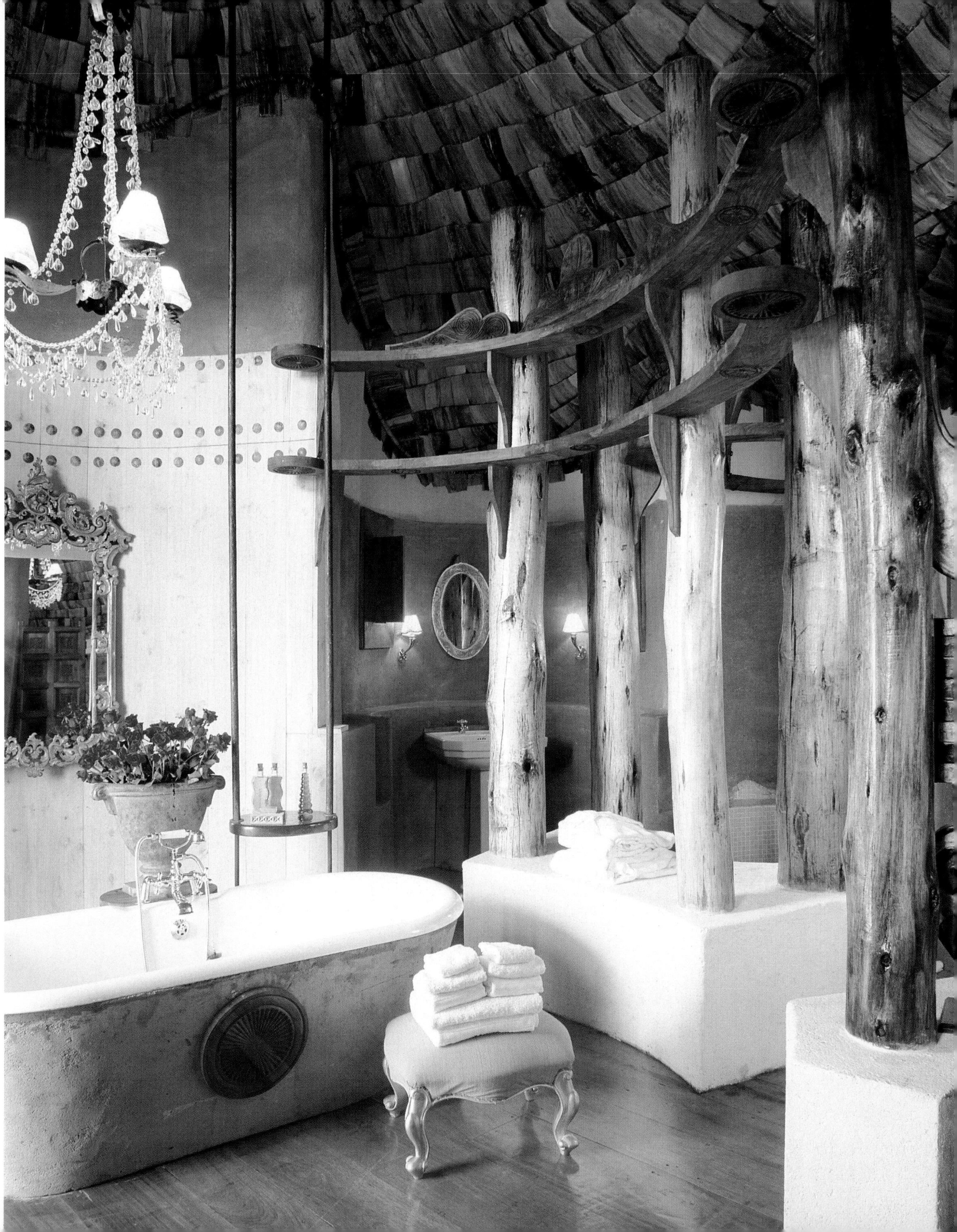

OPPOSITE

Even the bathrooms are not exempt from the "Masai Versailles" treatment. Each cottage has its own luxury bathroom, with a bath tub, shower, twin basins, and fittings imported from Europe. Terra-cotta pots carry bundles of red roses, Tanzania's signature flower.

LEFT & BELOW

The washrooms in the public areas are decorated with molded plaster panels, hand finished by artists on-site. They include a mix of antique and reproduction pieces, as well as ethnic African objects.

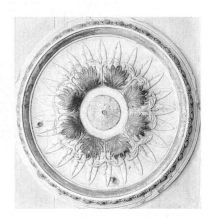

A B O V E   &   R I G H T

....

The king-sized beds were carved in Dar es Salaam and feature headboard frames covered in white taffeta, designed to softly reflect the daylight from the windows opposite. Suede bedcovers and silk organza cushions create a sense of decadent luxury, in sharp contrast with native African elements such as the clutch of Masai spears displayed in one corner of the room.

TREEHOUSE HIDEAWAY

A few minutes away from the house where Karen Blixen once lived at the foot of her beloved Ngong Hills, a latter-day pioneer has created a most unusual retreat. Unlike the colonial stone cottage of his celebrated former neighbor, Paul Verleysen has constructed a series of treehouses, designed to rise above the long Masai grass and surrounding bushland for unhindered views of the Ngong Hills. His idyllic existence here, running the treehouses as a lodge for safari guests, seems a world away from the pressures of the Belgian diplomatic service, which he left after more than twenty years to pursue an altogether different lifestyle.

Accommodation at Verleysen's lodge, Ngong House, is in one of four treehouses, built on stilts of local olive wood and with grass roofs made in the traditional African way. Each structure is two-storied, with a terrace, lounge and dining areas, and bathroom on the first level, and a bedroom on the second level. The houses are designed with comfort in mind, yet the interiors have a decidedly rustic feel. Walls and floors are lined in local timber, and furnishings are made from the wood of dhows salvaged from the coast. Verleysen designed and built each of the houses himself, drawing on the talents of regional artists and artisans to add many of the finishing touches, such as handwoven rugs, bedcovers, and cushion covers. Even the bathroom sinks are fired in a nearby pottery and painted by a local artist.

At sunset, the outlook from the treehouse terrace is spectacular. From this perch, fifteen feet above the ground, the panorama of the Ngong Hills fades slowly in the evening light, and the sound of lions can be heard close by. It is not hard to imagine Karen Blixen watching a very similar scene from her own veranda in the early years of her African adventure.

OPPOSITE

··

In each treehouse, a niche above the stairway to the living area is converted into a cozy sofa for reclining, reading, or just admiring the view beyond. Where windows do not have an outlook, they are filled with beautifully patterned Dalle de Verre.

ABOVE & RIGHT

....

In true safari tradition, evening meals are a special
occasion. After drinks around the campfire, guests can
enjoy an intimate dinner at their treehouse, where the
dining area is centered around a large fireplace. Much of
the table setting is produced by Kenyan artists and crafts
people. The crockery is fired and glazed locally, while the
glassware is made by the same artist responsible for the
Dalle de Verre windows. Only the silver cutlery, and
some of the wines, are imported.

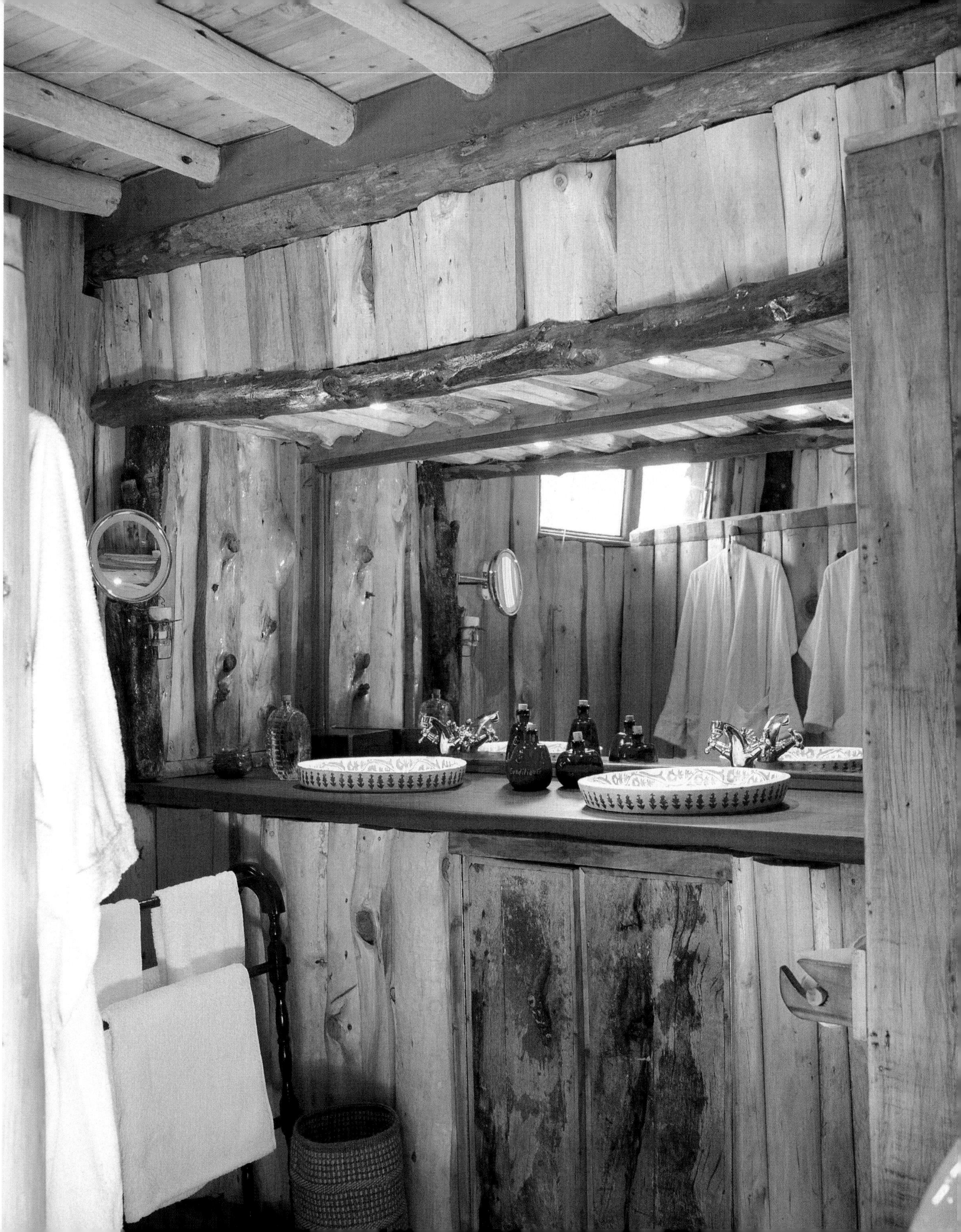

OPPOSITE

With their unfinished wooden walls, the treehouse bathrooms appear rough and ready, but a closer inspection reveals some luxury touches, such as fluffy white robes. The basins with shiny brass taps are made in a local pottery and painted by hand. Also handcrafted are the blue glass bottles and soap containers.

ABOVE

Twenty feet above the ground, the bedrooms have wonderful views over the treetops to the Ngong Hills. Each is decorated in a different style—in this treehouse the look is oriental. The four-poster bed is from Bali and is canopied with yards of fine mosquito netting. The bedcover is from India.

LEFT & ABOVE

....

Owner Paul Verleysen drew on his background as a
construction engineer to build the treehouses himself, an
undertaking that took a year and a half. One ingenious
feature is the entrance hatch, which closes automatically
with the help of attached weights. The ten-acre site
Verleysen chose for the lodge is a thirty-minute drive
from Nairobi, but feels completely isolated with its thick
bushland and abundant wildlife.

TWENTIES ELEGANCE

Few safari operators in Africa can boast a history as illustrious as that of Cottar's. Founded by American Charles Cottar in 1919, Cottar's 1920s Lifestyle Safari Camp recreates the grandest days of Kenya's colonial age. One look at the camp log book shows that few outfits are as qualified for the job. In 1924 Cottar's was the guide of choice for the Duke and Duchess of York's tour of East Africa. Two years later it was Woolworth Donahue and Babe White who called on the camp's services to take them hunting in style. Other famous guests include George Eastman and wildlife filmmakers Martin and Osa Johnson.

Today, the tradition of luxury camping continues under the watchful eye of the founder's grandnephew, Calvin Cottar. He has grown up in some of the wildest parts of Kenya and knows the African bush inside out. At the camp's site in the eastern Masai Mara, Cottar and his team of expert guides share their unrivaled knowledge of the area and wildlife with guests they lead on expeditions for game viewing, tracking, walking, bird shooting, or fly fishing.

For hedonists, the main attraction of Cottar's is undoubtedly the camp itself. Four spacious tents with high ceilings and timber floors are luxuriously furnished, with every detail true to the original, including the four-poster beds. Each en-suite bathroom contains a classic canvas bath, filled on demand with water that has been heated over a log fire to the preferred temperature. After a piping hot bath has washed away the day's dust, dressing in black tie is de rigueur for the camp's evening meal. Dining in the mess tent is silver service and by candlelight, with champagne and fine French wines to partner a gourmet three-course menu. Port and cigars complete a night redolent with the elegance of the past.

OPPOSITE

....

Each tent is furnished in a manner befitting royalty. Polished four-poster beds are made up with crisp white cotton sheets and handmade quilts filled with ostrich feathers. The covered porch is set with canvas-slung rocking chairs and a small table where afternoon tea is served. Luggage is transported in leather trunks and may include a complete safari kit made to order in advance. Brass lamps light the tent at night, when the only sounds come from the African bush.

ABOVE

A froth of fine muslin and mosquito
netting shrouds the four-poster beds,
while a handmade cotton lace spread and
pillow covers recreate the romantic mood
favored by Edwardian ladies on safari in
hot climes. The freestanding swing mirror
and folding tray table are other
hallmarks of colonial style.

OPPOSITE

The bathroom is a zipped compartment
within the tent. Although there is no
running water, facilities are far from
primitive. The bath, a canvas sling on a
folding wooden frame, is filled with hot
water on request. A porcelain sink,
handmade toweling robes, and mahogany
toilet seat are unexpected finds.

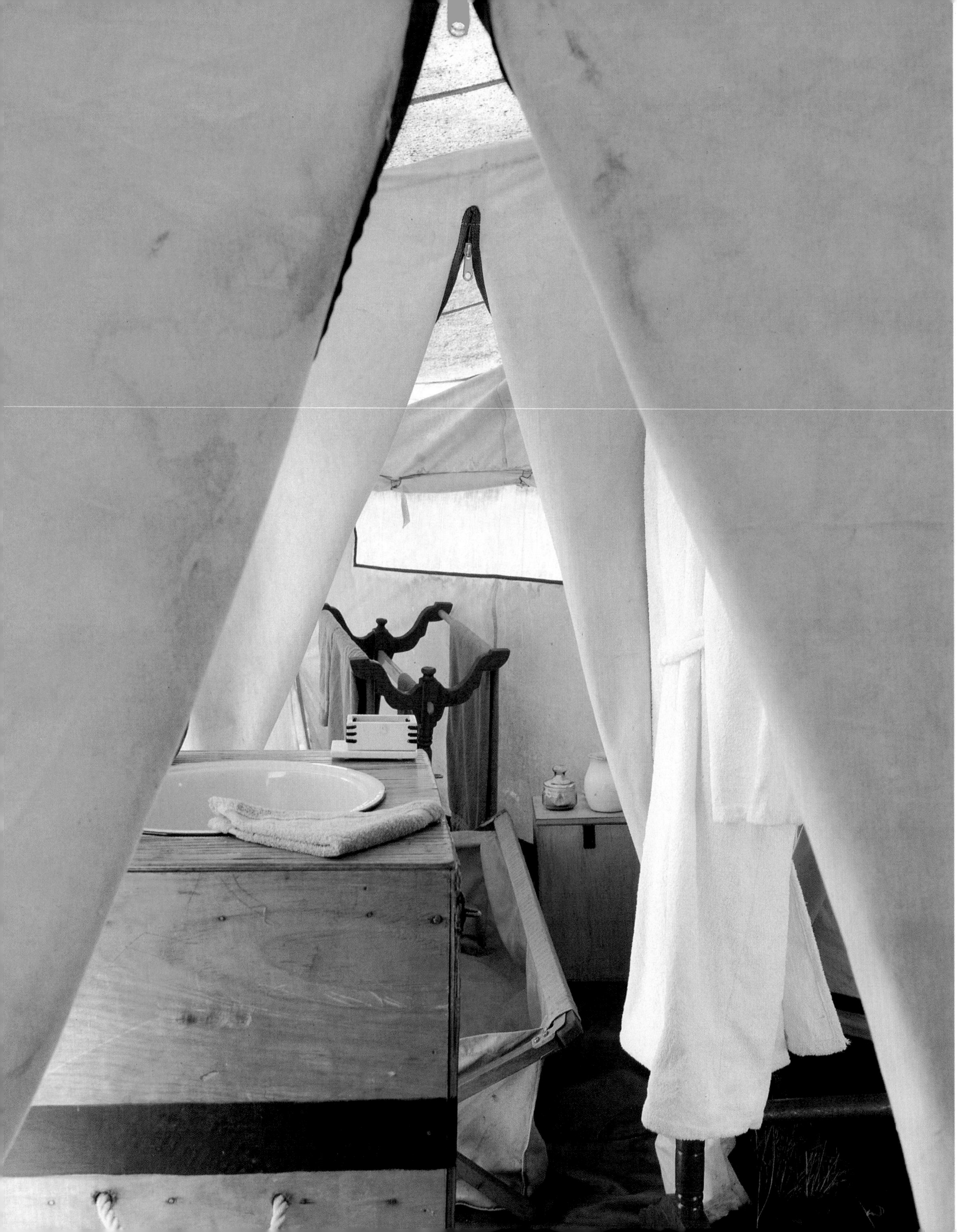

LEFT & ABOVE

....

Dinner is served in the open mess tent, or under the stars on especially warm nights. The meal is often based around meals served to famous guests from past safaris and might include fresh fish, glazed venison, or roast duck. The table is set with antique china, crystal glasses, and silver cutlery. Other authentic details include a 1920s gramophone and brass hurricane lamps.

ABOVE, LEFT & RIGHT

Cottar's is a four-hour drive south of
Nairobi, or less than an hour by private
plane. The camp sits in an exclusive
concession of 100,000 acres at Olentoro,
in one of the satellite ranches of the
Masai Mara Game Reserve.

OPPOSITE

With views over sweeping plains and
rolling green hills, the site is untouched
by any other tourism or development. The
tents are designed by Glen Cottar, one of
the founder's descendants, based on the
original 1920s Cottar's mobile camps.

SPLENDID ISOLATION

Remoteness was the quality that most appealed to veteran safari guide Richard Bonham when he came across a magnificent corner of northeast Kenya in the Chyulu Hills. The panoramic view over a vast plain to Mt Kilimanjaro, the rich wildlife, and the absence of tourism sold him on the location for both his home and lodge. It was the quintessential Africa, with flat-topped acacia tortillas trees and short-grass plains, golden in the dry season and green in the rainy. The downside was that water would have to be hauled 170 miles to serve the site. Undaunted, Bonham undertook a year of negotiations with the Masai elders of the Chyulus to win a concession for three hundred acres. The idea was to create a home, but also take in a handful of paying guests.

The focus of home and lodge life is the main "mess," which serves as both dining and lounge area. Accommodation is in individual thatched cottages, designed with open facades so that guests in bed have uninterrupted views of Kilimanjaro and the savanna below dotted with lions, cheetah, giraffe, and zebra. In the absence of a front wall, each of the cottages is raised on stilts to provide security from wild animals that come too close.

As the location is so isolated, Bonham had no choice but to use building materials that could be found nearby. Rocks and boulders were used for construction of the walls. Timber for the main trusses and building frames was collected from the area, but only fallen trees. The cluster of lodge buildings that comprise Ol Donyu Wuas—the main mess, five thatched cottages, and Bonham's own house—are designed to be as open as possible. Furnishings are kept simple so that attention is focused on the scenery, fulfilling Richard Bonham's aim that guests feel part of the view rather than simply acting as observers.

OPPOSITE

The furniture in Bonham's own bedroom, like the rest of the lodge, is made from natural materials found on-site. The bed and dressing table are fashioned from a fallen olive tree. Blue mosquito netting, purchased at the fabric bazaar in Nairobi's Biashara Street, adds a shot of electric color. Blue and white rugs from Guatemala carry through the color theme.

RIGHT

There are some thirty-four species of large mammal on the concession, of which elephants form a significant group. A local carving on an interior doorway is a reminder of their presence on the plains below.

BELOW & OPPOSITE

Due to the lodge's isolated location, minus the usual tourist bustle, encroaching wildlife can be a real threat. Bonham keeps rifles on hand in the event of danger, from top: a 416 Rigby rifle, a 20-bore Beretta, and a 12-bore Cogswell Harrison.

LEFT & ABOVE
....

Richard Bonham's living room is an impressive textural mix of natural elements and native art. Both the sofa and dining table were made at the lodge from fallen olive trees, and the upholstery and cushions are in hand-painted fabric from Zimbabwe. The floor is paved with natural stone slabs from Mombasa, and the roof is thatched with coconut palm leaves. Other objects of interest include the straw hats from Mombasa and a silver tea service that belonged to Bonham's grandfather.

ABOVE, LEFT & RIGHT

*Nothing stands between guests and the
view they enjoy from their private
balcony. A tray table stands at the ready
for a cooling sundowner, and also
provides display space for a native bowl
containing mementos of wild Africa.*

OPPOSITE

*Each of the thatched cottages is designed
so that the views can be enjoyed while
lying in bed. The cottages look directly
out onto a forest of acacia tortillas, with
open savanna and the volcanic peak of
Mount Kilimanjaro in the distance.*

CHAPTER TWO

UPCOUNTRY
LIVING

TENTED REFUGE

Journalist Dominic Cunningham-Reid is considered eccentric by many of his friends. Despite the fact that his mother is an interior decorator who has renovated several luxurious homes, Cunningham-Reid prefers the freedom of living in a tent. Since childhood he has been fascinated by the idea of the camp tent: its proximity to nature, its simplicity, and its sense of portability. Now, as a television correspondent covering trouble spots around Africa, he has chosen a tent as his home.

The tent sits surrounded by bushland in the midst of a giraffe sanctuary in Larengai, about ten miles from Nairobi, where giraffes and warthogs are among his most frequent visitors. But despite its wild setting, the tent is a far cry from the usual collapsible kind. It was designed and built by Cunningham-Reid to be sturdy enough to serve as a permanent base, and large enough to accommodate a few favorite pieces of furniture, like his king-size bed made from Burmese teak. A platform of cedar serves as the floor, with a framework of metal poles and cedar posts providing support for the canvas walls and thatched roof. Windows of mosquito netting are positioned so that the view outside can be seen while lying in bed. The bathroom has running water and is housed in a separate structure built of river rocks. Cunningham-Reid has no need for a kitchen—he either cooks over a campfire or eats at his sister's house, the only other habitation on the reserve.

With his deluxe tent, which also includes electricity and internet connection, Cunningham-Reid has established a lifestyle to match his needs exactly. As he spends ten months of the year in war-torn parts of the continent, he finds it essential to come home to a tranquil spot where he can live simply and unwind from the pressures of his job.

OPPOSITE

··

Taking pride of place in the tent is an eight-foot bed made from Burmese teak. The precious wood came from a boat carrying a cargo of tea, which was wrecked off the Kenyan coast. Cunningham-Reid waited for the tide to bring the wood ashore, then collected it and made the bed himself with the help of his brother-in-law.

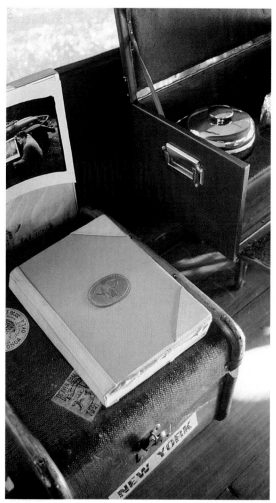

ABOVE, LEFT & RIGHT

*With little space for furnishings,
Cunningham-Reid has had to choose his
pieces carefully. The trunks are from the
1920s and provide storage for clothes, as
well as a surface for displaying
mementos and photographs.*

OPPOSITE

*A study in one corner of the tent
comprises an English oak desk and filing
cabinet from the 1930s. The brass shell
casings on the floor are from a Soviet
tank and were collected while on
assignment in the Sudan.*

AFRICAN ORNAMENTAL

Rising from the Kenyan savanna like a futuristic mud hut, the brainchild of American Alan Donovan is in every way a reflection of Africa's traditional architecture, design, and applied art. The structure itself houses one of the world's finest collections of African crafts, amassed by Donovan over a period of thirty years. First sent to Africa by the U.S. State Department during Nigeria's Biafran war, Donovan fell in love with the continent and stayed—not as a government bureaucrat, but as managing director of African Heritage, Kenya's most successful Pan-African art gallery. His passionate interest in native architecture and craft led him to the towering mud mosques of Mali, the painted mud houses of Ghana, the mud castles of Southern Morocco, and the coral buildings of coastal East Africa. All of these provided inspiration for his monumental home, set on eight acres overlooking Nairobi National Park.

Although the house appears to be made from mud, it is in fact built of hand-hewn stone blocks covered with a layer of tinted plaster. Its sturdy construction enables it to better withstand the rainy season than the typical mud house. Diverse decorative elements are evident, from the West African designs on the exterior walls to the protruding wooden poles and turrets, typical of the traditional mud mosque.

Inside, an intense combination of color, pattern, and texture delivers a dramatic vision of African culture. Textiles, carvings, and furniture—collected from across the continent or commissioned from artisans—make the house as much a handicraft gallery as a space for living. The home boasts such a diverse collection that Donovan intends it to be preserved as a museum on his death, demonstrating to succeeding generations the practical beauty of Africa's indigenous arts.

OPPOSITE

....

The pool house is thatched with makuti *palm leaves, typical of roofing along Africa's eastern coast. Hanging from the ceiling are three pendant lamps fashioned out of traditional fish traps from Kenya and Madagascar. The long sofa is covered with a tribal fabric from Mali called* bokolofino.

ABOVE & RIGHT

··

Each of the terraced levels offers views over the plains of
Nairobi National Park with its roaming herds of giraffe,
zebra, ostrich, and wildebeest. The hand-carved chairs
on the upper terrace are from Lamu, with cushions of
Mali mud cloth and Bakuba pile cloth from Congo-Zaire.

LEFT & ABOVE

The rooftop sitting room, used for sundowners and
parties, is a favorite of Donovan's. The walls and
ceilings are hand-painted with designs based on the
geometric patterns of mud cloth from Mali. Displayed
against the wall, in between framed Bakuba cloths,
is a collection of walking sticks and spears from
Zaire, Kenya, and Tanzania. Functional African crafts,
like the wooden fruit bowls set out on a Masai cowhide,
are a popular motif throughout the house.

The graphic nature of African arts and crafts is used to dramatic effect in the living room. The double-sided sofa in the center of the room is made from a baby cradle from Lamu, and is covered with Mali mud cloth. On the back wall, two beaten metal panels by a contemporary Nigerian artist depict Yoruba folk tales.

An intricately carved Indian screen serves as a backdrop for a display of African and Indian textiles, collected over many trips around both continents. The silver and ivory horn is from Guinea. Next to the screen is a circumcision mask of brass appliqué on wood. It is worn by boys of the Marka tribe in Mali.

The house displays traditional and contemporary crafts from all over Africa. A wrought-iron table and chair in the side entrance are modern pieces made at Donovan's African Heritage gallery. The beaded wall-hanging in the shape of a lizard depicts the god of thunder, and came from a Nigerian Shango priest. Beside the swimming pool, a Masai shield makes a bold statement.

B E L O W

Keeping watch from the roof is a contemporary statue of a warrior from the Acholi tribe in Uganda, created by African Heritage artist John Adochameny.

OPPOSITE

Decorating the living room are clusters of African artifacts, like these painted Wakamba beer gourds from Kenya, used for dowry payments. The groom's father presents the gourds, full of the local brew, to the bride's family.

ABOVE

One end of the rooftop sitting room features wall decoration based on a Masai shield design. The sofa and cushions are covered in Mali mud cloth. Intricately embroidered Bakuba cloth trails over a four-poster bed from Lamu.

MOORISH MISCHIEF

There are two landmarks synonymous with Kenya's scandalous Happy Valley set. One is the Muthaiga Club, where they gathered for polo afternoons and drunken cocktail parties. The other is a Moorish fantasy palace on the shores of Lake Naivasha, built by Major Cyril Ramsay-Hill and his wife Mary in 1926, the year after their arrival in Kenya. No expense was spared to build the domed mansion, which was based on Ramsay-Hill's grandmother's house in Seville. Marble was brought from Tanganyika for the columns supporting the arched colonnades around the courtyard, floor tiles were imported from Spain, and antiques from France.

The exotic atmosphere quickly attracted the pleasure-loving Happy Valley crowd for weekend-long soirees. Mary is said to have enjoyed reclining naked in her sunken bath with a glass of champagne, while guests gathered round her to chat. It may have been on one of these occasions that she cemented her love for Josselyn Hay, Lord Erroll, the playboy who was later murdered in a case locals referred to ominously as "white mischief." Mary's long-suffering husband chose to turn a blind eye to their liaison, but the house became so renowned for its free-flowing gin that it was later dubbed "the Djinn Palace."

In the mid-1960s, long after the party set had disappeared, the Djinn Palace was bought by June and Hans Zwager with a view to restoring the decaying mansion and turning it into a small hotel. The two-and-a-half-year undertaking involved complete refurbishment of the original hardwood floors, teak doors, and crumbling walls. But by the time the Zwagers had brought the palace back to pristine condition, they were so entranced with both its physical grandeur and intriguing past, they resolved to keep it for their home.

OPPOSITE

....

Although the overall theme of the house is Moorish, its eccentric former owners added some unusual touches. Major Ramsay-Hill insisted on installing an enormous fireplace in the living room, copied from an English farmhouse. The large portrait above the fireplace is of Molly Ramsay-Hill, whose home in Seville was the model for the Naivasha house, and whose money paid for it.

An authentic taste of Moorish Spain in Africa: the tiles decorating the courtyard were made in Seville in 1926 especially for the house. The doors are of Burmese teak and were made by Punjabi artisans who had come from India to work on the Uganda Railway in the 1890s.

Even though Kenya had its own marble quarry at the time Ramsay-Hill was building the house, he ordered the marble for the courtyard columns from Tanganyika. He is said to have had numerous samples made until he was happy with the slenderness and grace of the columns.

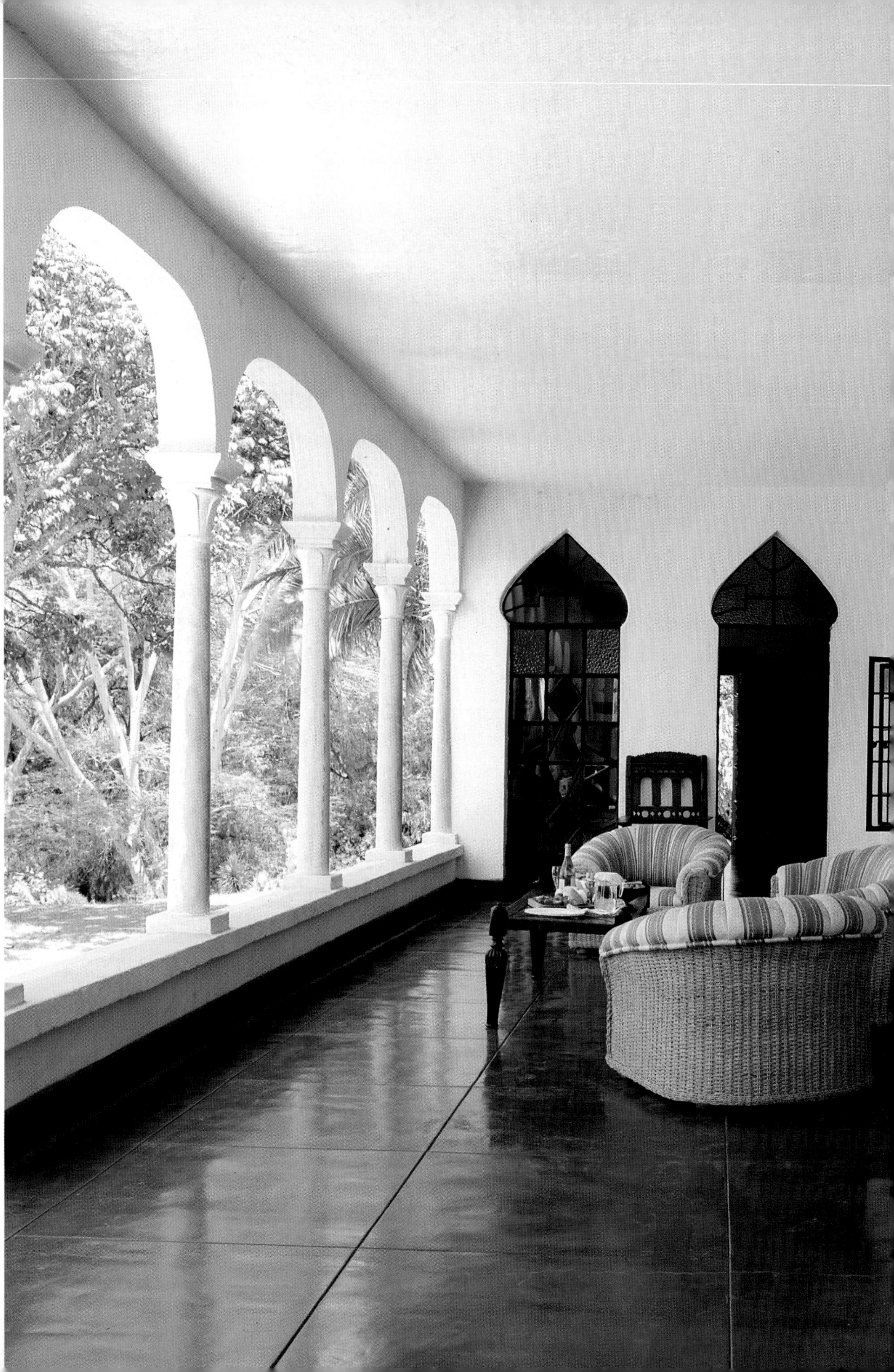

LEFT & ABOVE

···

Unlike most traditional Spanish houses, Ramsay-Hill's creation was not walled in. The view of Lake Naivasha and the trees edging it were so delightful that the major wanted to make sure they could be seen from the long balconies he built around his palace. Also atypical are the minaret and dome, which are more in keeping with Arab mosque architecture.

ABOVE & RIGHT

....

*On completion, the house and 5,000-acre estate
surrounding it was named Oserian, meaning "place of
peace" in the Masai language. Its tranquil appearance
now belies the boisterous scenes once played out here by
the colorful characters of the Happy Valley crowd. Guests
reputedly indulged heavily in both pink gin and erotic
pleasures. In the case of the latter, they might simply
wander out into the courtyard or grounds to indulge if
none of the five bedrooms were free.*

LEFT & ABOVE

....

Present owner June Zwager has given the interior scheme of the living areas a decidedly bohemian flavor. She wanted to decorate the home in a manner befitting the grand scale of Oserian and settled on a mix of fabrics and furnishings from India, France, and Africa, adding color and pattern to the enormous rooms. The original Sevillian tiles feature throughout the house, with hand-painted fragments used in a mosaic commemorating the completion date of the house.

POLISHED PERFECTION

By the shores of Lake Naivasha, Dodo Cunningham-Reid continues the grand English tradition of building follies. Inspired by the whimsical structures built by nineteenth-century aristocrats in her husband's native Britain, Cunningham-Reid devised plans for her own twentieth-century folly. Such disregard for convention came as no surprise to her husband, whose stepmother was Diana, Lady Delamere, of Happy Valley notoriety.

The soaring folly began as a series of rough sketches and evolved over four years into a monument to Kenya's wide open spaces and rich natural resources. The completed eight-storied tower stretches 115 feet into the treetops, with each of the levels boasting views of the lake and the Aberdare mountains.

What may have seemed an outlandish venture in her native Germany, was possible in Africa largely due to the ready availability of the quality timbers required for the project. The steel frame of the pagoda is clad in cypress, and the interior richly paneled with African hardwoods. Cypress was used for the floors and ceilings, and mahogany for the paneling in the kitchen, lounge room, and dining rooms.

Despite the exterior impression of a fairytale fortress, the tower's living areas have been devised by Cunningham-Reid to provide a relaxed and calming environment for the couple's weekend escapes. From the lounge room on the lower level to the tiny meditation room at the top, the interior scheme has been carefully thought out, with much of the furniture made locally to Cunningham-Reid's specifications. The mood is overwhelmingly romantic, with lots of special touches—crystal vases full of roses in every room and crisp white linen on the magnificent beds—recalling the spirit of colonial luxury.

OPPOSITE

....

As the tower is octagonal in shape, the walls take on some rather quirky angles, particularly near the top of the structure. This small guest bedroom is dominated by a huge French antique bed.

ABOVE & RIGHT

....

Although the completed tower looks idyllic in its natural setting, the surrounding wildlife caused havoc during construction. Plumbing pipes had to run deeper than usual to prevent hippos crushing them underfoot when they emerged from the lake, and birds had to be chased from the structure's steel skeleton to stop them nesting.

LEFT & ABOVE

....

*The unifying interior element is the generous use of
wood. In the lounge room, the walls are paneled with
mahogany. To stop the mahogany looking too dark,
Cunningham-Reid color-washed the panels with three
layers of color: terra cotta, light yellow, and white, and
rubbed them down with sandpaper between each coat.*

OPPOSITE

*Cunningham-Reid drew on the skills of local carpenters
and artisans for much of the interior decoration,
including the paneled walls and the mahogany dining
table. The chairs, designed by Marc Rampelberg,
are made of olive wood and inlaid with ebony.*

RIGHT & BELOW

*In place of a conventional staircase, stairs in the style of
a ship's ladder link the upper floors. Near the top, this
tiny meditation room provides space to unwind.*

ABOVE

The master bedroom, high in the tower,
is Cunningham-Reid's favorite room.
It contains just three pieces of furniture:
a desk, chair, and French nineteenth-
century bed. From here she has views
through the fever trees to the lake.

OPPOSITE

Cunningham-Reid describes her style as
unconventional yet timeless, a description
that aptly fits the bathroom. Its cypress-
lined ceiling and marble-paneled walls
are classic, while the leopard-print
lamp shades add a whimsical touch.

MODERN ROMANTIC

I n his idyllic forest home, artist Tonio Trzebinski has combined the romance of living in the Kenyan wilds with a strong contemporary design sensibility. Enjoying the rare luxury of being able to create a home from scratch, he was able to indulge both his artistic passions and a love of African nature he has fostered since childhood.

When he came across an untouched plot of forest for sale, surrounded on three sides by a nature reserve and just twenty-five minutes drive from Nairobi, Trzebinski jumped at the chance to buy it. He and his wife, Anna, started designing a house straightaway, envisaging a natural retreat where their children could roam free, waking to the sound of the forest birds and falling asleep to the sound of rain on a corrugated iron roof, so reminiscent of Trzebinski's own childhood experience.

The house is built along classical lines on two levels, with a large, open communal living space downstairs, bedrooms upstairs, and an attic at the very top. Although the building itself is made from inexpensive concrete breeze blocks, the exterior is faced with weatherboard, left unpainted to harmonize with the bush environment.

Having spent much of his early life on safari, Trzebinski has imbued the interior of his home with the textures of the great African outdoors. The floor of the living area is a magnificent stretch of polished Elgon olive wood covering thirty square feet. This creates a beautiful base for the modern elements that characterize Trzebinski's style. Gleaming stainless-steel columns provide structural support for the room as well as lending an urban edge. Here, as throughout the house, abstract works of art in earth tones mix with rugged timber furnishings and fine fabrics to create a seamless blend of the natural and luxurious.

OPPOSITE

....

Tonio Trzebinski's multiple talents as artist, sculptor, craftsman, and builder are evident in the expansive ground-floor living area. Tables, chairs, light fittings, sofas, lamps, and blinds are all made on the premises to the artist's specifications. The large canvases hanging on the walls change constantly, as existing works are sold to friends and visitors and replaced with new ones.

ABOVE

A stairway leads from the living area to
the bedrooms upstairs. Trzebinski set out
to make it a striking centerpiece,
constructing the railings and support
beams from driftwood collected while
surfing off Kenya's Indian Ocean beaches.

OPPOSITE

The open-plan living area was designed
to provide space for displaying the artist's
paintings, and is large enough to
incorporate a library, lounge, dining, and
dancing areas. It can easily accommodate
thirty or more guests at parties.

....

*Without compromising the modern edge of their home,
Tonio and Anna Trzebinski have achieved an
undoubtedly romantic mood for the master bedroom. The
drape of the sheer netting over the bed, ruffled
pillowcases in country cotton checks, and subtly marbled
wall treatment are the perfect foil for the mahogany
floors and rough-hewn edges of the timber bed.*

ABOVE & RIGHT

The cedar verandas that edge the house upstairs and downstairs are a favorite spot for relaxing in the sun. The upper veranda off the bedrooms faces east toward a forest of olive, fig, and acacia trees. Giraffe are often visible feeding on the acacia, while more than 250 bird species nest among the dense foliage.

OPPOSITE

The guest bedroom includes elements of safari style—the folding camp chair, delicate bed linen, and mosquito netting—as well as bold modern touches such as the abstract canvas by Tonio Trzebinski.

OPPOSITE

Tonio Trzebinski makes furniture, art, and sculpture to sell, as well as for his own use, and so his house functions as a kind of gallery. As furnishings are sold, new pieces are made to replace them. Common to all his creations is a strong sense of wild Africa, and many of his materials are gathered from the bush.

ABOVE, LEFT & RIGHT

This coffee table is one of the artist's most popular pieces, and can be found in collections as far afield as Spain, Italy, England, the U.S., and Indonesia. A shallow tray is built into the table and topped with a fitted sheet of glass to provide a display area for artifacts, found objects, or safari mementos.

ENGLISH ECCENTRIC

It is a measure of the British influence that once gripped East Africa that pockets of transplanted English life can still be found there. Hiding in the trees at Hippo Point, on the shores of Kenya's Lake Naivasha, is one such example, a mock-Tudor farmhouse built in the style made fashionable in Edwardian England by architect Edward Luytens. With its romantic Tudor gables and cottage rose garden, the house would not look out of place in 1930s Wiltshire or Kent. It was discovered in ruins by Anglophile designer and decorator, Dodo Cunningham-Reid, who has restored its former charm and reinvented it as a graciously appointed guest house.

Cunningham-Reid has carved out a name for herself in Kenya as an interior designer with great natural flair. She cut her teeth on the Lake Naivasha Hotel, owned by husband Michael Cunningham-Reid, and when the couple eventually sold up, she immediately turned her sights to other building and design projects to occupy her creative talents. One of her first major undertakings was the construction of her own lakeside home, an octagonal eight-story tower. With her 1930s Tudor farmhouse, which sits on an adjoining piece of land, she has again made a distinctive mark, combining the classic and the quirky.

The exterior cedar beams, once covered in thick black paint, have been stripped back to their original state, as have the wooden surfaces inside. The interior scheme mixes refined European colors and antique furnishings with handmade objects and fabrics. The overall effect is of a comfortable English cottage with modern aspirations. It is only when guests walk through the garden to the lake, where hippos play in the shallow waters, and antelope, gazelle, and zebra come to drink, that the true identity of this romantic hideaway is revealed.

OPPOSITE

....

The three-gabled Tudor farmhouse was built in the 1920s and '30s in the popular romantic English style of the period. Cunningham-Reid dramatically overhauled the interior space to create eight bedrooms and bathrooms, also converting the stables and a pigeon house into elegant accommodation. The house now serves as a base for upmarket safari guests.

OPPOSITE
Originally a windowless garage, the airy drawing room underwent a complete transformation. It features two fireplaces, carved on the premises from local wood, nineteenth-century French antiques, and large contemporary canvases by artist Tonio Trzebinski.

LEFT & BELOW
Decorative objects are functional yet classic, recalling the luxury of colonial days. An ingenious invention of Cunningham-Reid's, the bamboo frame holding petite glass bulbs, serves as a vase for roses from the garden.

ABOVE

A side table in one of the bedrooms

supports a charming collection of curios

and objects. The vase is of handblown

glass, set into an iron basket, and was

made by a local artist; the silver piece

is an antique collapsible traveling cup;

and the gilded carving in the shape of a

pineapple supports a bedside lamp.

OPPOSITE

Stripped cedar beams punctuate the pale,

color-washed walls of the bedrooms.

Furnishings, mostly French antiques, are

kept to a minimum, with the decorative

focus on the antique fabrics used for the

bedcovers and curtains. The cushion

covers are printed with African designs

and were sourced locally.

CLASSIC COLONIAL

Tristan and Lucinda Voorspuy live surrounded by a significant piece of colonial Kenyan history. Their picturesque stone house, Deloraine, was built in 1920 by one of East Africa's most charismatic figures, Lord Francis Scott. The younger son of the 6th Duke of Buccleuch, Scott was working for Britain's Viceroy in India, Lord Minto, when he fell in love with his chief's daughter, Lady Eileen, and decided to make a fresh start for himself and his new bride in Kenya. The house he built, on farmland in the highlands above Nairobi, was constructed by Indian laborers in the colonial style popularized by the British in India. It was here, in his spacious two-storied home with views over the Rift Valley, that Scott could take time out from the rigors of his governmental post.

The Voorspuys acquired the house in 1992, when the death of then-owner Pam Scott, daughter of Lord Francis, brought the property onto the market. They envisaged it as the ideal base for their burgeoning horseback safari business. First, however, the couple faced the daunting task of making major structural repairs. The results of their work are beautifully evident now in the neatly tiled roof and sturdy exterior stonework, the pristine whitewashed walls of wattle and daub inside, and the polished woodwork throughout.

The generous proportions of the rooms have made furnishing them the biggest decorating challenge. To help fill the vast central drawing room downstairs and the huge bedrooms upstairs, the Voorspuys have acquired some impressive pieces of furniture, some of which are antiques from Tristan's family home in England. In keeping with the grand tone of the interior, portraits of Lord Francis and Lady Eileen grace the main living areas, keeping watch over their former domain.

OPPOSITE

....

When the Voorspuys bought Deloraine in 1992, little had been done to the house for twenty years. In addition to giving the walls a bright white finish, replacing existing paintwork in murky colors, the couple paid great attention to returning the wood surfaces to their former shine. The mahogany floors are typical of colonial homes of the 1920s.

ABOVE & RIGHT

....

*The wonderfully elegant master bedroom would look
equally at home in a grand English country house.
Formerly the nursery for Lord Scott's two daughters, Pam
and Moy, the Voorspuys have transformed the room into
a handsome, light-filled space. They find it the ideal
place for unwinding on return from horseback safaris.*

Originally painted a murky yellow from floor to ceiling, the walls of the drawing room are now a pale primrose, with a white border left at the top to emphasize the cedar-beamed ceiling. Lord Francis's portrait hangs above the bookcase.

The drawing room is dominated by an enormous stone fireplace, an original feature of the house. The furnishings are a mix of Kenyan pieces and English antiques, including a collection of framed equestrian prints.

LEFT & ABOVE

....

*An elevated veranda runs along the front of the house,
and is often used as a dining area for breakfast and
lunch. Wicker-backed planters chairs and a sofa provide
seating for evening drinks. The veranda looks out onto
ten acres of garden, originally farmland run by the
previous owner, the daughter of Lord Francis.*

INDIAN IMPRESSIONS

About ten miles north of Nairobi, swathed in fields of fragrant coffee beans, stands a sprawling bungalow with its origins firmly planted in the early architecture of colonial Kenya. In the century or so since it was constructed, the house has had just three owners, each preserving the integrity of the original structure, but at the same time lending their own subtle sense of style.

Kogeria, as the house is known, was built in 1904 by an Englishman, John Ellis. Transplanted to Kenya from India, he brought with him the distinctive house style of the British in India, designed to evoke the coziness of an English country cottage, yet adapted in both its features and materials to the local climate. Built from Kenyan granite with interior walls fashioned largely from daub and wattle, its most extraordinary attribute is the lofty seventeen-foot-high ceilings that help to keep the rooms cool. This was typical of colonial homes in India and soon became the norm in Africa, as did the sweeping veranda. At Kogeria the deep veranda encircles the bungalow, in effect creating an additional living space where inhabitants can enjoy cool afternoon breezes while admiring the view.

Several decades after Ellis constructed the house, it passed into the hands of Tony Fenwick who farmed the acreage with coffee beans, as did many of the settlers in the area, Karen Blixen most famously among them. Then, in the early 1960s, Fenwick took the then unusual step of selling off his land in twenty-acre plots, enabling native Kenyans to become smallhold farmers. The house was sold to a Swedish couple, African-born safari operator Ulf Aschcan and his partner Marianne Nilson. Together they have imbued the house with an exotic flavor in keeping with the building's Indian origins.

OPPOSITE

....

The color scheme for the sitting room takes its cue from the earth tones of Africa, from the golden brown of the dry savanna to the deep red worn by Masai tribes. The overall effect is of an exotic desert tent, with walls lined in northern Indian textiles and Persian carpets covering a floor of mahogany parquet.

OPPOSITE

The veranda is seventy-two feet long,
providing ample room for separate
outdoor dining and living areas, perfect
for afternoon naps or entertaining.
The dining table and leather-covered
safari chairs are made locally.

ABOVE

Marianne Nilson has lent the home its
distinctive interior scheme, much of it
centering on the use of textiles. Together
with a small group of women she makes
furnishing fabrics to order, weaving each
length using hand-dyed cotton thread.

OPPOSITE

The long, low dining table is made from a tree that toppled over in the garden. The floor cushions are covered in handwoven fabric designed by Marianne.

RIGHT & BELOW

Following in the best traditions of colonial living, the Aschans make an important occasion out of the evening meal, setting the table with the best porcelain, crystal glasses, silver cutlery, and a bowl of fragrant roses.

ABOVE & RIGHT

....

The house is thought to be the first in the district to be built in stone. Although most of the building materials were sourced locally, the hardwood for the door and window frames was imported from India. Likewise, the grounds are planted with a mix of native trees, such as wild fig, croton, and Nandi flame trees, and non-indigenous trees including jacaranda and frangipani.

ITALIAN INVENTION

Over a thousand miles from her native Italy, in a leafy Nairobi suburb, interior designer Marinella De Paoli has created an oasis of serenity informed by the classical spirit of her homeland. The house is set on three acres of grounds that once formed part of a coffee plantation. The only reminders of that origin today are the enormous Rosslyn trees that flank the main driveway and the lush grounds studded with groves of native African trees. The house itself is a bungalow built in the 1960s, and was in a terrible state of repair when De Paoli stumbled upon it in the search for a home for herself and husband, Franco. Captivated by the magical gardens, she was convinced she could transform the unappealing house into an inspired living space.

The premise behind the transformation was that the home should be in harmony with its surroundings, allowing the colors of the garden to filter through. To that end, De Paoli retained the minimalist style of the original house, putting in place a simple interior scheme designed to complement the building's modern lines. She left most of the windows unadorned so that the forest of trees can always be glimpsed.

Thoughtful touches of color and texture add warmth to an otherwise spare interior. In the dining room, plain white walls provide the backdrop for a pair of dining tables, handpainted by De Paoli to simulate green marble. In the master bedroom, a sky blue ceiling brings a sense of the outdoors inside. The bedhead, also painted by De Paoli, echoes the theme, as does the bathroom with its blue marble fittings. All the rooms have been kept free of clutter. A few beautiful pieces of furniture or a special work of art are all that are needed to complete De Paoli's vision for a perfectly balanced home.

OPPOSITE

··

The stone-clad floor continues outside to a large
terrace, divided into summer living and dining areas.
The terrace is surrounded by jungle-like foliage,
comprising avocado and banana trees, grevillea palms,
jacaranda, and frangipani. This fragrant forest supports
numerous bird species, including sunbirds, doves, and
weavers. The De Paolis regularly spread seed out
on the pergola to lure them down from the treetops.

LEFT
....

The lounge room with its beamed ceiling and graceful arches would not look out of place in a Tuscan farmhouse. Marinella De Paoli wanted to give the impression that the house had existed forever, mixing elements of Italian and English country style.

OPPOSITE

A fireplace dominates the dining room. This one, and those elsewhere in the house, are carved in stone according to a seventeenth-century Italian design. Part of the couple's collection of Venetian glassware is set out on the handpainted dining table. The lamp shade hanging above is from a Maharaja's palace.

ABOVE

The living area features a wall of full-length windows, repeated above on the gallery level. The room has been kept intentionally free of color, allowing the greens of the garden to filter through instead. The window surrounds throughout the house are stone-dressed using an old English technique.

....

Although the house is a modern structure, De Paoli used
her skills as an artist to give the interior an antique feel.
In her daughter's bedroom she treated the walls with a
color wash-and-wax technique to age them. The bed
echoes the antique mood, with a bedhead handpainted
by De Paoli, and the fabric for the bedcover and
cushions handwoven by a local craft cooperative. The
writing desk is a seventeenth-century piece from Italy.

ABOVE & RIGHT

....

The clean white spaces of the interior are full of light,
with both the lounge and master bedroom on the level
above featuring a wall of windows looking out to the
garden. A staircase made of local mvuli *wood leads*
from the bedroom to De Paoli's design studio.

ABOVE LEFT

To disguise a rather ugly corridor leading to the guest wing, De Paoli camouflaged the door at the end with a trompe l'oeil scene of an iron door opening on to trees beyond. It is intended to give the impression of leading out to the garden.

ABOVE & OPPOSITE

The master bathroom is clad in tiles of local blue marble and the walls painted in a Venetian style called marmorino. *A bowl of rare African gold beads and cuffs from Ethiopia, Somali, and Yemen inspires De Paoli, a jewelry designer.*

CHAPTER THREE

COASTAL
RETREATS

PARADISE ISLAND

Few destinations in the world offer a glimpse of paradise as unspoiled as Mnemba Island. A tiny private atoll off the north-east coast of Zanzibar, Mnemba is fringed by white sands that edge a clear green lagoon, fed by the Indian Ocean. Tropical fish dart among the coral reefs, which stretch for over ten miles, providing a habitat for a rich diversity of marine life. Closer to shore, dolphins bask in the shallows, and sea turtles lay their eggs on the pristine beach. This protected marine reserve is the stunning setting for Mnemba Island Lodge, owned by Conservation Corporation Africa.

In keeping with the environmental significance of the island, the lodge itself is built almost exclusively from natural materials, and is solar-powered. The resort comprises ten self-contained beach "huts" facing the lagoon. Spread far enough apart in the thick tropical foliage to ensure complete privacy, each of the huts has its own secluded bathroom, as well as a shady veranda for whiling away the hours reading or simply enjoying the view out to sea.

A barefoot stroll through the jungle-like vegetation leads to a spacious open-air lounge and dining area, where low-level seating with plump cushions wraps around a sweeping stone ledge. The walls are made of flexible palm matting, rolled up under a high thatched roof to allow cooling breezes to waft through. This communal gathering place provides an escape from the midday sun, a relaxed environment for sundowners, fresh mango and papaya juices, or ice-cold champagne at any time of day or night. Whether here in the lounge, in the private huts, or wandering the perimeter of the island, there is nothing save the sound of African birdsong and the lapping of the lagoon waters to encroach on Mnemba's idyllic isolation.

OPPOSITE

....

Cool and serene, the main living area creates an informal mood in keeping with the island's laidback pace. The color scheme echoes the outside view of a white sandy beach, translucent water, and brilliant blue sky. The carved wooden furnishings are from the neighboring island of Zanzibar.

ABOVE

Each beach hut has its own veranda, protected from the sun by deep overhanging eaves. Tea, coffee, and home-baked biscuits are served here every morning before breakfast. Simple day beds offer a place for afternoon siestas.

OPPOSITE

The huts are built from natural materials such as palm leaves and local wood. Bold fabric stripes create a colorful border around windows, doors, and around the walls. The gap between the walls and roof allows air to circulate freely.

LEFT & ABOVE

....

Water sports on Mnemba Island take many forms.
Some guests prefer to stray no further than water's edge,
beachcombing for beautiful shells, or simply drinking in
the view. The more energetic can choose from snorkeling
over miles of coral reefs, diving, swimming with
dolphins, sailboarding, or big-game fishing. As the island
has never been settled, used only by fishermen as a
haven from storms, the beaches are completely unspoiled.

ABOVE

Apart from the rainy season, when the
resort closes from April through June,
the weather on Mnemba is blissful, with
hot sunny days and balmy evenings. As
the island is situated just a few hundred
miles from the equator, the sun sinks
quickly as evening approaches. Dinner
is usually served under a clear sky.

OPPOSITE

As night falls, a table is laid out on
the lagoon shores, illuminated by torch
flames and hurricane lamps, and setting
the scene for an evening feast under the
stars. Along with tropical fruit and spicy
Zanzibari vegetable dishes, the meal
comprises freshly caught fish and lobster,
baked in a barbecue pit dug on the beach.

SULTAN'S PALACE

Zanzibar was once the heart of the nineteenth-century Spice route between the Arab world and India. On the back of this flourishing trade the island developed into a prosperous port attracting an exotic mix of inhabitants comprising native islanders and mainland Africans, Indian merchants and artisans, British and Portuguese traders, and, ruling over them all, the Omani Arab Sultans of Zanzibar. It is fitting, then, that the grandest of all the island's resorts is owned by a modern-day Arab sultan, the Aga Khan.

The Serena Inn is the Aga Khan's second venture on the island, a project aimed not only at firmly establishing the island as a luxury tourist destination, but also reviving its great cultural legacy. The inn is housed in two historic seafront buildings in Zanzibar's Stone Town: one, a turn-of-the-century colonial telecommunications building; the other, an old Arab residence, occupied by the British Consul during the 1940s and '50s. Before the conversion of the two adjoining structures could begin, an extensive restoration program was launched to return the buildings to their former glory. The Aga Khan's team surveyed and documented the existing interior and architectural features, before undertaking a detailed reconstruction.

One of the major challenges facing the restorers was finding artisans with the skills to reproduce Zanzibar's unique style of decoration, an eclectic melding of Arab, Victorian English, and Indian elements. Carpenters and plasterers were brought from India, mainland Tanzania, and Kenya to work alongside the handful of Zanzibaris who still practice the traditional island craft of wood carving. Once the basic structural restoration was completed, the two buildings were ready for transformation into a romantic retreat.

OPPOSITE

....

The Serena Inn is situated on the waterfront at the edge of Stone Town, overlooking the Indian Ocean. It perches on the seawall built by the Sultans of Zanzibar in the early nineteenth century to protect the port, and the sand foundation of its buildings, from the encroaching sea. Restoring the wall to its former strength was therefore a vital part of the hotel project.

ABOVE, LEFT & RIGHT

Detailed drawings of the original Arab house—thought to predate Stone Town itself—formed the blueprint for reproducing features such as windows and doors. Elements such as the wall lamps were adapted to suit modern needs.

OPPOSITE

A shady colonnade is characterized by thick white supporting columns. The architectural device is typical of the Arab world, as is the geometrical glass mosaic above, which is not only decorative but helps to soften the harsh African sun.

LEFT & ABOVE

....

The finished effect of the restoration is magical, combining Arab exoticism and colonial grandeur with the natural beauty of fragrant frangipani trees, a white sand beach, and the clear green waters of the Indian Ocean. Dhows, identical in style to those navigated by Arab traders along the Spice route last century, still sail the waters around Zanzibar.

ABOVE, LEFT & RIGHT

Some of the hotel's features and furnishings are original, tracked down from far-flung corners. Brass work and furniture brought from Pakistan and Afghanistan recreate the look of a wealthy Arab merchant's home.

OPPOSITE

Many of the interior details in the main reception area are reproductions based on illustrations or antiques. The ceramic floor tiles are typical of the nineteenth century and were made specially in England and Kenya to decorate key areas.

OPPOSITE

Rooms are decorated in typical Zanzibari style, drawing on influences from India, Persia, and Victorian England. Particular attention has been paid to internal finishes, drawing on the traditional skills of local artisans.

LEFT & BELOW

All the bedrooms at Serena face the ocean, most with their own private balconies overlooking the beach. Handcrafted slatted wooden shutters are adjustable and can be slanted to follow the sun's path during the day. Intricately carved antique furnishings also attest to the skills of Zanzibari carvers.

ZANZIBAR SPICE

Stone Town was once the grand capital and main trade port of the spice island of Zanzibar, a small and beautiful city of narrow winding lanes, palm-filled courtyards, mosques, traditional island houses, and elegant palaces. On a bright summer's day the effect is dazzling as the sun reflects off the distinctive white stone mansions and lime-washed buildings with their overhanging balconies and intricately carved window shutters and doors. In the midst of this enchanting labyrinth, hotelier Emerson Skeens has created an exotic environment that recalls the romance of eighteenth-century Persia.

The hotel Hurumzi is a melding of two historic buildings that have been merged into one fantastical palace combining Persian, Indian, and Arab elements. The back part of the hotel dates from the 1840s and is built in the style of the Omani Arabs who governed Zanzibar. The more elaborate section at the front is the former mansion of Tharia Topan, a rich Indian merchant who served as financial advisor to Sultan Barghash, last in the line of ruling Arabs. In keeping with his position, Topan's house featured massive beams of Burmese teak and handsomely carved windows, doors, and interior details.

The original features of both buildings have been lovingly restored by Skeens. He masterminded the architectural restitution and joining of the two structures as well as the interior scheme. Skeens makes no apology for the Arabian fantasy he has concocted within Hurumzi. Its rich colors and textures reflect the Eastern Persian style developed by the Moghuls, who carried it into India and Pakistan. The furnishings are antiques from different periods in the island's history, and the color scheme is also traditional, with periwinkle blues, jade greens, purples, and pinks evoking the splendor of old Zanzibar.

OPPOSITE

....

Dinner at Hurumzi takes a page from the Arabian Nights. *The rooftop terrace has an exotic Arab-Swahili character, with a Zanzibari menu served under a canopied roof. Guests unwind on giant appliquéd pillows to watch the sun setting over Stone Town. As the light fades, candles are lit in traditional brass lanterns.*

RIGHT & OPPOSITE

Each of the bedrooms incorporates an eclectic array of Zanzibari features. The stained glass above the shuttered windows in this bedroom is an original feature of the house. The exotic bed that dominates the room belonged to a wealthy merchant in the 1930s. Its unusual construction, with netting suspended from a frame, is designed to accommodate a ceiling fan.

BELOW

Zanzibar culture has been strongly influenced by the presence of Indian traders and artisans. This cabinet is thought to have been brought to the island from Gujarat.

LEFT & ABOVE

....

The jewel colors, rich Indian silks, and ornately carved furnishings in this bedroom conjure up images of the Arab Sultans that ruled Zanzibar in the eighteenth century. Skeens has intentionally created a mood of romantic sensuality, which perhaps explains why guests tend to spend most of their time in the bedrooms.

ARABIAN REFLECTIONS

Not far from the Kenyan coast where Arab merchants sailed their trading dhows on the way to Zanzibar, an exotic Moorish residence stands testament to their influence. The house was built at Kilifi Creek in the 1940s from solid blocks of coral, hewn by hand and cemented together with mud. The coral structure wore well over the years, but by the time George and Philippa Corse bought the house in 1989 the roof and interior were in complete need of renovation.

Rather than just restore the two-storied house to its original state, which featured a decidedly European facade, the Corses decided to transform it into an Arab-style mansion. Inspired by the ruins of a nearby palace dating from the sixteenth century, Philippa Corse knocked through many of the internal walls to create several large, airy rooms overlooking a central courtyard and colonnaded patio. The plain rectangular windows that once punctuated the rooms were given a Moorish treatment with pointed tops and wooden shutters. Arches, a flat crenelated roofline, and brilliant white walls washed with lime completed the exterior picture.

Inside, the original high ceilings have been retained with their rough-hewn beams of wood from the *mvuli* tree, now protected by law. For the floors, terra-cotta tiles from Mombasa provide a cool surface underfoot. Much of the furniture, both in the main living room and on the veranda, was made especially for the house in the local style, an adaption of the cabin furnishings of English ships that came to East African shores in the nineteenth century. The bedrooms, too, have been decorated with furniture carved by Kilifi carpenters using Kenyan hardwoods, the beds themselves draped in mosquito netting and upholstered with mattresses of coconut matting.

OPPOSITE

··

Looking at the Corse's immaculate Arab home now, it is hard to believe it was once derelict, with a roof eaten away by insects. Renovation has been a slow process. Working without an architect, they rebuilt the house bit by bit using local builders to interpret their ideas. The finished home is beautifully simple, with spacious living areas inside and outside, bright whitewashed walls, and structural details in African hardwoods.

Although the house originally had a European facade, it was built by an Arab and always featured an Arab-style layout, including a central courtyard. The Corses heightened the effect with a Moorish treatment of the windows and colonnade, as well as limewashed walls. A sprinkling of palms and a lily pond with goldfish provide the finishing touches.

ABOVE

The vast living area upstairs was achieved by knocking down several interior walls. The sofas and armchairs are reproductions of nineteenth-century furnishings in the coastal style, featuring distinctive tapered and scored legs. The wall lamps are copies of those made by the renowned carvers of Lamu Island.

OPPOSITE

Mosquito netting is essential in the bedrooms because of the threat of malaria. Here, the netting shrouds a single bed carved by a local carpenter. The four-poster is designed with bands across the top to support the canopy of netting. The mattress, stuffed with coconut matting, is also handmade.

LEFT

....

The household spends most of its time on the veranda,
which is set up permanently as a lounge area thanks to
its sheltered position. The furniture is made locally from
African hardwood, and the open-weave seats and backs
of the sofas and chairs are made in the regional style
with cotton string in place of wicker.

TROPICAL SECLUSION

T he coast of Kenya is edged by some of Africa's most beautiful beaches. Rows of towering palm trees, long stretches of white sand, and clear, blue-green water are the magnet for weekenders from Nairobi or Mombasa or vacationers from abroad. The oceanfront town of Malindi has already blossomed into a resort, as have other areas along the coast. Those in search of seclusion and unspoiled beaches need to look further afield to find tranquility, like the owner of this house, who guards its location jealously.

With the help of her brother, the owner set about building her dream vacation home in 1987, after selling her house in now-bustling Malindi. She used no architect's plans, simply her own sketches and pictures clipped from magazines. Also crucial to the project was an Indian builder from Mombasa who was skilled in many of the traditional building techniques of Africa's coastal architecture. Under his watchful eye, the house was constructed from blocks of coral, which were then whitewashed, and roofed with a thatch of coconut palm leaves. As there was no electricity in the area, the pace of building was painstaking, progressing one room at a time.

For the interior, the owner wanted to combine a relaxed mood with local character, in keeping with the beachside lifestyle. Her solution was to look to Kenya's past. In the coastal city of Mombasa she scoured derelict buildings, slated for demolition, in search of precious hardwood. She uncovered a wealth of Indian teak, imported to Kenya in early colonial days, as well as furniture, architectural features, even bathroom sinks. This imaginative recyling has enabled the owner to surround herself with an array of beautiful objects and textures, made all the more appealing for their sense of history.

OPPOSITE

....

Echoing the fuss-free decorative scheme used throughout the house, the kitchen looks pristine with its white-washed walls and scrubbed wood benches. There are no extraneous details, and everything in the room has a practical purpose, in line with the owner's belief that a vacation home should be kept free of distractions, and be as easy as possible to maintain.

RIGHT

The open-plan living space features double-height ceilings and a gallery level overlooking the dining area. On the art deco table, bought in Malindi, traditional African digos—*food covers woven from palm leaf—serve both a practical and decorative function.*

OPPOSITE

Most of the wood used in the interior has been recycled from other sources. The banisters are made from timber reclaimed from demolition sites around Mombasa, while the sofa is fashioned from an antique bedhead carved by the bajuni *artisans on the island of Lamu.*

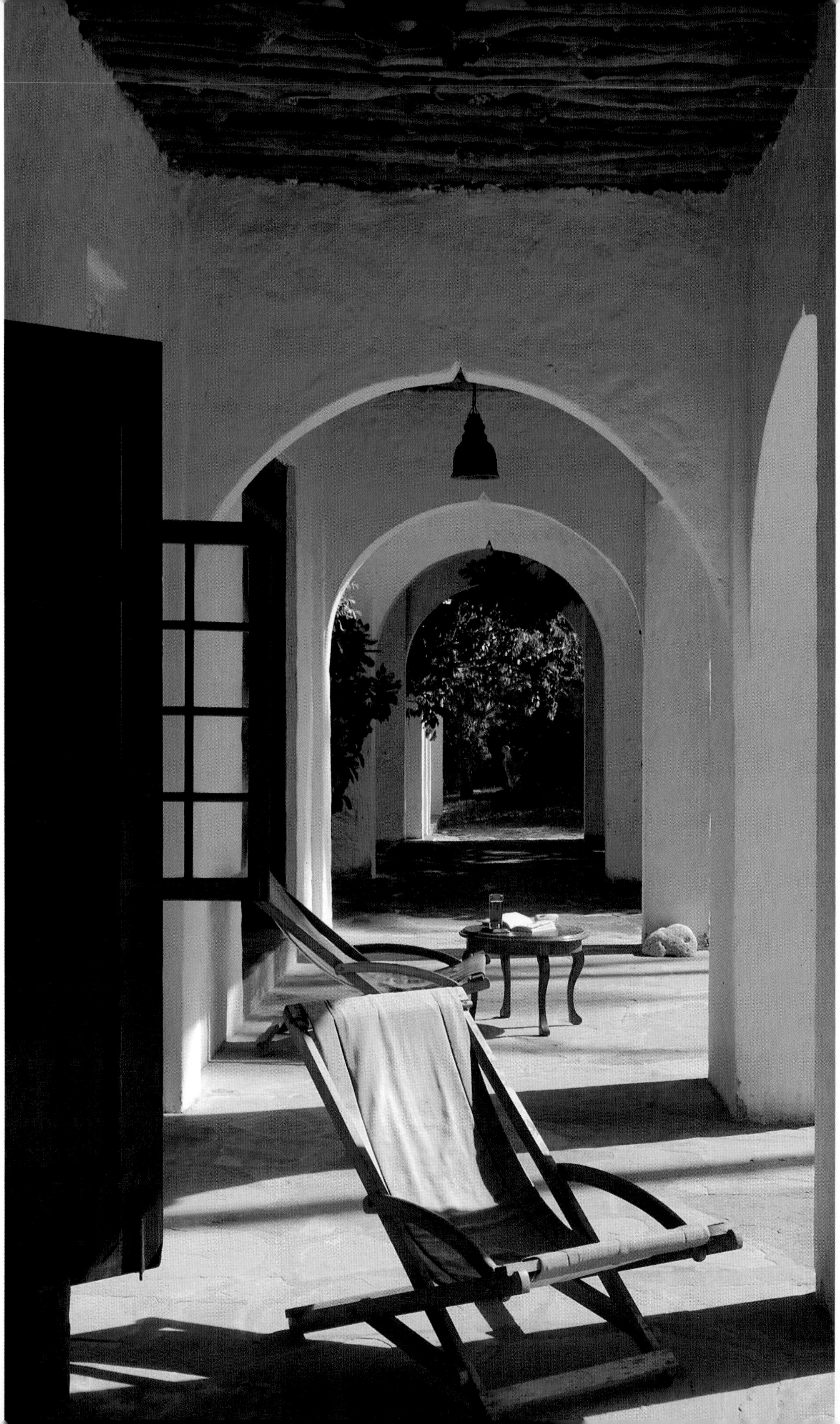

ABOVE

The appeal of this bedroom lies in its monastic simplicity. The carved four-poster bed and printed bedcover provide the only surface decoration. Windows are kept free of drapes, as much for effect as ease of maintenance.

LEFT & ABOVE

....

The traditional thatched roof is made from thick
swatches of dried leaves from coconut palms, which are
bound tightly to an intricate timber framework, creating
a surprisingly waterproof shelter. The furniture on the
veranda is also made in the traditional style of the
coastal region, and scattered with cushions in bright
prints, a mix of African and Western designs. Here, as
elsewhere in the house, the floor is paved in local stone.

SWAHILI SPIRIT

Lamu Island is a tiny speck in the Indian Ocean, once a stop on the prosperous trading route of the Arabs. Little seems to have changed in this remote part of Africa since the seventeenth century when it was a hub of Swahili culture. It was this exotic and untouched quality that had drawn Robert and Fiona De Boer to the island for years, and eventually persuaded them to buy a majestic home by the beach, Kisimani House. The house was once part of the estates of a wealthy nobleman, the Kalif of Zanzibar, and has been studied by archaeologists, anthropologists, and architects for decades, all intrigued by its traditional features and the insights it offers on Swahili culture.

The five-story mansion is constructed around a sunken central courtyard, with large, open-plan rooms reflecting the communal nature of ancient Swahili life. Intricate decorative plasterwork and carved details give the interior a magical quality, particularly on the ground floor where the harem was once housed. Much work has gone into restoring the interior and exterior features to their former splendor. The existing three-story house needed replacement of all the structural timbers, restoration of the plasterwork, and installation of electricity and running water. Once the basic elements were in place, designer Rob De Boer evolved plans for another two stories, which now blend seamlessly with the originals.

The De Boers traveled widely in the Islamic world to glean inspiration for their project, and this influence has been carried through to the interior decoration. Typical of Islamic homes, the courtyard is the focus of household life. At Kisimani it has been adapted to use as a dining terrace, with a profusion of greenery providing shade during the day, and an open roof providing impossibly romantic views of the starlit sky at night.

OPPOSITE

··

A bedroom suite recreates the feel of a Swahili harem, with the bed enclosed by curtains of sheer muslin netting. The decorated banas, *or roof joists, are original features, and are typical of seventeenth-century Swahili architecture on Lamu Island.*

ABOVE, LEFT & RIGHT

Furnishings are made in the Swahili style, with the emphasis on comfort and durability. The niches above doorways traditionally provided space for displaying treasure such as porcelain bowls, decorated plates, and silverware.

OPPOSITE

In the entry hall, as elsewhere in the house, the ceilings are constructed using durable mangrove poles. The walls are built of coral blocks up to half a meter thick. Door and window frames are made from bomba kofi, *an exotic hardwood.*

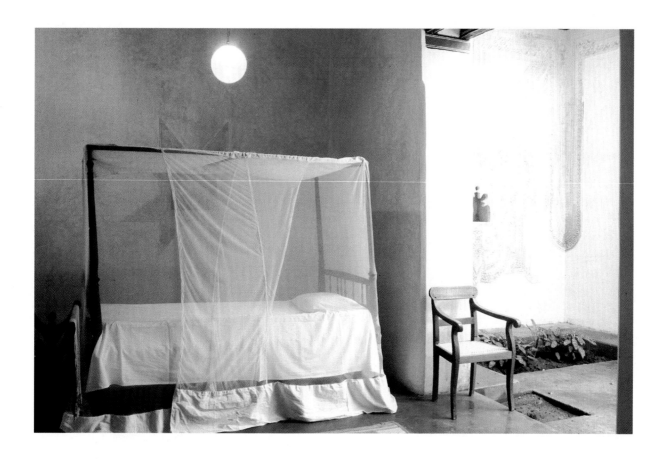

OPPOSITE

The ground-floor level with its elaborately carved plasterwork, once contained the harem. It looks out onto a central courtyard, where a single palm grows up through the house. This area was the setting for important ceremonies such as weddings, traditionally marked by a week of feasting, music, and dancing.

ABOVE

Adjoining the harem on the ground floor are two seventeenth-century msana, *meaning "long chamber room" in Swahili. They are marked by elaborate patterns on the plaster-coated walls, and by niches with dense carving in the shape of stylized turtles. The chambers now make cool, airy bedrooms.*

A B O V E   &   R I G H T
....

*Stairs lead up through the central courtyard of the house
to the terrace on the first floor, where a mass of
bougainvillea offers shade and color. Household life
tends to focus on this open-air living area, which
provides padded banquettes for relaxing, and a dining
table and chairs made by Lamu woodworkers.*

SAFARI GUIDE

ABERCROMBIE & KENT Tailor-made safaris for individual travelers, encompassing a wide variety of luxury camps and lodges.

> *Sloane Square House,*
> *Holbein Place*
> *London SW1W 8NS*
> *tel: 020 77309600*
> *fax: 020 77309376*

LUCA SAFARI LTD Luxurious private tented safari in the Chyulu Hills of southern Kenya.

> *P.O. Box 236*
> *Mtito Andei, Kenya*
> *email: lucasafari@softwork.it*

GALDESSA CAMPS LTD Romantic campsite in Kenya's largest national park. *(as featured on page 24)*

> *P.O. Box 15095*
> *Nairobi, Kenya*
> *tel: 254 2 890635*
> *fax: 254 2 891307*
> *email: geneva@galdessa.com*

TORTILIS CAMP Exclusive tented lodge on the edge of the Amboseli National Game Reserve.

> *P.O. Box 39806*
> *Nairobi, Kenya*
> *tel: 254 154 22551/2*
> *fax: 254 154 22553*
> *email: chelipeacock@attmail.com*

KITICH CAMP Six luxury tents in a lush oasis in the Mathews mountains, Samburu, Kenya.

> *Bush Homes of East Africa*
> *P.O. Box 56923*
> *Nairobi, Kenya*
> *tel: 254 2 571647/571661*
> *fax: 254 2 571665*

OL DONYO WUAS Private game ranch with a cluster of five thatched cottages high in the Chyulu Hills. *(as featured on page 70)*

> *Richard Bonham Safaris Ltd*
> *P.O. Box 24133*
> *Nairobi, Kenya*
> *tel: 254 2 884475*
> *fax: 254 2 882728*

CRATER LODGE
Extravagant lodge with baroque-style interiors, overlooking the Ngorongoro Crater. *(as featured on page 40)*

Conservation Corporation Africa
P.O. Box 74957
Nairobi, Kenya
tel: 254 2 750298
fax: 254 2 750512

MASHADO TENTED SAFARI
Camp in Tarangire National Park, southeast of the Serengeti.

tel: 254 2 606231
fax: 254 2 606234
Email: mashado@form-net.com

SAND RIVERS
Riverside camp in Tanzania's Selous wilderness.

Richard Bonham Safaris Ltd
P.O. Box 24133
Nairobi, Kenya
tel: 254 2 884475
fax: 254 2 882728

MNEMBA ISLAND LODGE
Exclusive private island off the coast of Zanzibar. *(as featured on page 162)*

Conservation Corporation Africa
P.O. Box 74957
Nairobi, Kenya
tel: 254 2 750298
fax: 254 2 750512

COTTAR'S 1920S LIFESTYLE SAFARI
Twenties-style tented safari camp on the Kenyan-Tanzanian border.

P.O. Box 44191
Nairobi, Kenya
tel: 254 2 884508
fax: 254 2 882234
email: Cottars@form-net.com

HIPPO POINT
Tudor-style house on the shores of Lake Naivasha, available for private rentals. *(as featured on page 126)*

Hippo Point House
P.O. Box 24930
Nairobi, Kenya
tel/fax: 254 2 891621

SERENA INN Luxury oceanfront hotel in restored historic houses in Zanzibar. *(as featured on page 170)*

> P.O. Box 4151
> Zanzibar, Tanzania
> tel: 255 54 33587
> fax: 255 54 33019

NGONG HOUSE Individual treehouse accommodation at the foot of the Ngong Hills, a half-hour drive from Nairobi. *(as featured on page 54)*

> P.O. Box 24963
> Nairobi, Kenya
> tel: 254 2 891856
> fax: 254 2 890674

KISIMANI HOUSE Swahili-style private home on the island of Lamu, available for rental. *(as featured on page 202)*

> P.O. Box 24711
> Nairobi, Kenya
> tel: 254 2 882409

HURUMZI Boutique hotel converted from an Arab merchant's house in Stone Town, Zanzibar. *(as featured on page 180)*

> P.O. Box 4044
> Zanzibar, Tanzania
> fax: 255 54 33135
> email: emerson@zanzibar.org

ILNGWESI LODGE Rustic-style lodge in the hills of Northern Kenya, built and run with the involvement of the local Masai community.

> Ian Craig
> P.O. Box 24513
> Nairobi, Kenya
> tel: 254 2 607197
> fax: 254 2 607893

OFFBEAT SAFARIS Small-scale horseback safaris based at the comfortable colonial residence, Deloraine. *(as featured on page 132)*

> P.O. Box 56923
> Nairobi, Kenya
> tel: 254 2 571647
> fax: 254 2 571665

BORANA LODGE Classic safari lodge comprising five "bush" cottages overlooking Mount Kenya. *(as featured on page 32)*

> P.O. Box 24397
> Nairobi, Kenya
> tel: 254 2 567251
> fax: 254 2 564945
> email: ras@swiftkenya.com

PREVIOUS PAGE: *Rope bridge at Ilngwesi Lodge*
OPPOSITE PAGE: *Poolside at Ilngwesi Lodge*
THIS PAGE: *Netted beds at Serena Inn*

INDEX

*Page numbers in italics refer to
illustrations, on which information
will be found in the captions*

ACKNOWLEDGMENTS

The publishers would like to thank the following for their kind assistance: Abercrombie & Kent, Robin Schiesser and Danita Wright at Architectural Digest, Caroline Brooke-Johnson, Dionne Waters, Juanita Carberry, Kathini Graham, the Natural History Museum in Bern, David Stogdale, Theresa Pereira and Chris Brown at Conservation Corporation Africa, Pierre-André Mourgue D'Algue, John Warburton-Lee, Luca Belpietro. Special thanks to all those who kindly allowed their homes, lodges, and camps to be photographed, and apologies to those whose homes we were unable to include.

Color Reproduction by David Bruce Imaging.

Picture Credits Architectural Digest: U.K. edition cover, 32, 35, 37, 84, 87, 88, 90, 91, 92, 95, 108-115 Courtesy Architectural Digest © 1997 The Condé Nast Publications. All rights reserved. Used with permission. Getty Images: 22; Glasgow University Archives: 15; Hulton-Getty Picture Library: 10, 11, 14; Juanita Carberry: 18-19; Kathini Graham: 16tr; Natural History Museum Bern: 13; Pierre-André Mourgue D'Algue: 26; Royal Commonwealth Society Collection, by permission of the Syndics of Cambridge University Library: 12, 16bl, 21; Royal Geographical Society © Phillips Atlas: 7; Still Pictures © Muriel Nicoletti: 78; Trip Photographic Library © H. Rogers: 160. African symbols throughout from: African Designs From Traditional Sources, Dover Pictorial Archive Series, Dover Publications.

I have been visiting this part of Africa for many years now and have always thought there was an interesting book to be made on the private houses, lodges, and safari life of this very beautiful part of the world. Producing a book such as this is time-consuming, risky, and very expensive so I am grateful in the first place to Beatrice Vincenzini for responding to my initial proposal so positively and in taking up the challenge of the project when all she had to rely on was what I told her.

The photographs have been taken over a number of years but mainly in one long trip in 1997 and another in early 1998 which was blighted by the most appalling weather Kenya has experienced for nearly 20 years, destroying bridges, swamping roads and generally making travel around the country, especially to the remoter parts, virtually impossible. So it was a shame not to get Lewa and Kuki Gallmann's Retreat, among others, for this reason.

I would also like to mention and thank the following who helped in many different ways – Air Kenya (which kindly provided return flights to Lamu), Halvor and Shasti Astrup, Mike and Sheila Barker, Rogue and Peggy Barkas, Anthony Cazalet, Michael and Minnie Cecil, Chris Flatt, Iver and Patsy Hecktorman, Murray Levet, Boo Mellowes, Dodo Cunningham-Reid, and to all the owners of houses, lodges, and camps who let me in to photograph. I must sincerely apologise to the few who kindly allowed me to photograph their homes but for reasons beyond my control were omitted in the final edit. I would like to give a special thank you to Brian and Annie Macoun whose house in Karen we were lucky enough to be able to use as a base when not on photographic trips.

Lastly, thanks to Sophia with all my love. **Tim Beddow**